WHY
YOU
CAN
GO
OUT
DRESSED
LIKE
THAT

MODERN FASHION
EXPLAINED

 Thames & Hudson

Marnie Fogg

CONTENTS

CHAPTER ONE
FANTASY
10

CHAPTER TWO
DISPLACEMENT
56

INTRODUCTION
MARNIE FOGG

The history of fashion is marked by rebellion: the more radical the change, the stronger the opprobrium against early adopters. Each significant moment of transition hinges upon the throwing of new outré shapes by avant-garde protagonists, who have undermined the traditional notions of volume and fit, introduced ideas of displacement, challenged the ideals of male and female beauty or fashioned a new fantasy identity.

Why You Can Go Out Dressed Like That champions the improbable, the provocative, the uncomfortable, even the seemingly ridiculous. Inspired by diverse sources, theories and concepts, as well as by the development of futuristic textiles and techniques, the book explores the work of designers who strive to extend the boundaries of their imagination and creativity. It is a misapprehension that to be fashionable hinges upon mindless adherence to imposed patterns of dress. Indeed, in order to make clothing eloquent or outspoken, it is necessary to expose such patterns as démodé. *Why You Can Go Out Dressed Like That* explains how ignoring set precedents is both powerful and contentious. Divided into five chapters—Fantasy, Displacement, Provocation, Distortion and Volume—the book identifies and analyses the designs that most tellingly represent each concept.

Fantasy fashion is distinct from fancy dress and costume. At the turn of the 20th century, Paul Poiret eschewed the rigidity of structure and overt femininity that dominated the period and tapped into the fantasy of the Arabian nights to introduce into mainstream fashion his lampshade tunic dress and other designs of Eastern influence. Later, Paco Rabanne used innovative construction techniques to create his chain-link dress, which represented a break from the formality of the 1950s and the hourglass figure, and became a symbol of youth and the triumph of science over nostalgia.

Fashionable fantasy allows the wearer to enhance their identity in ways that exaggerate and expand upon their innate characteristics without taking on another persona. When Bob Mackie designed outfits for Cher in the 1980s, such as the showgirl costume, he captured the essence of Cher and exploited it. Likewise, Dolce & Gabbana's designs ensured that Kylie remained Kylie in spite of her Aphrodite robes. Occasionally, fantasy fashion is used by groups to define their status: in Japan, youth subculture is influenced heavily by teenage girls who adopt certain styles of dress, such as Sweet Lolita, based on historical and cartoon trends.

Displacement is fashion's answer to Surrealism. Founded in the 1920s by French writer and poet André Breton, Surrealism subverts inanimate objects and places them in a new, unsettling context. In fashion, the most obvious example of displacement is the transposition of the inside of the body to the outside, with bones, muscles and the circulatory system appropriated by designers as surface decoration. In the 1930s, influenced by Surrealist artist Salvador Dalí, Elsa Schiaparelli applied an image of the upper part of the human skeleton to an all-black evening gown. Since then, variations have appeared in numerous collections, including menswear by Katie Eary, and as stage costumes, such as the skeleton corset worn by pop diva Lady Gaga. Displacement in fashion has also allowed British design duo Boudicca to offer a glimpse of a dystopian future, creating a world in which protective clothing is deemed a necessary accoutrement to survival.

It is important to distinguish between garments that feature objects as ornamentation, such as the typewriter dress by Mary Katrantzou and the augmented anatomies of Thierry Mugler's automotive corset dress, and those garments that fully adopt an inanimate identity, such as the hair dress by Maison Martin Margiela, which summons a feeling of unease, and the umbrella dress by Agatha Ruíz de la Prada, which evokes only humour. Displaced materials such as paper have also been used regularly to make clothes: the 1960s witnessed a trend for throwaway paper dresses; later, Hussein Chalayan constructed his 'Ventriloquy' collection from sugar glass in his anti-consumerism manifesto.

In contemporary fashion, it has become increasingly difficult to spark a reaction to the wearing of provocative dress. There is an almost limitless tolerance of the wider reaches of perceived decency: the outrage caused by the near nudity of singer Josephine Baker in the 1920s and by the topless bathing suit of US designer Rudi Gernreich in the purportedly permissive 1960s is now reserved for those insensitive to religious or cultural taboos. What was once perceived as risqué—the Playboy bunny with her corseted figure and pneumatic breasts, wearing the now-iconic uniform of the nightclub waitress—is rendered a tired cliché and perceived as quaintly old-fashioned, an attitude that is symptomatic of changing aesthetic and sexual values. In the 21st century, a sense of irony is necessary to promulgate female stereotypes with conviction, evidenced by Jeremy Scott's fur bikini worn beneath a transparent plastic raincoat and Pam Hogg's streamlined Catwoman all-in-one subverted by a three-dimensional rectangle for a hat.

Shifts in the erogenous zones, always the subject of various theories and debates, reveal parts of the body previously concealed or deemed shocking. Alexander McQueen's bumster trousers, with a low rise that reveals the top of the buttocks, changed the cut of trousers for more than a decade. Provocation is not necessarily sexual: fashion has long been used to disseminate revolutionary ideas, seen in the nihilism of Vivienne Westwood's punk T-shirt in 1977. When Lady Gaga bound raw meat to her body with butcher's string in 2010, in a suggestion of flayed flesh, it gave a whole new meaning to red-carpet dressing. Commonly, the red carpet is an arena for provocative dress, seen in the barely there dresses by Julien Macdonald and the extreme cut-outs of Ashish's sequin dress.

Generally, the boundaries of the human body are adhered to by fashion designers, with all the salient points—breasts, waist and hips—acknowledged with varying degrees of accuracy and intent. These variations may lead to the subtle readjustment of the silhouette, exemplified by the striped silk peplum on David Koma's summer dress and jacket, and the architectural origami shapes evident in Louise Goldin's knitwear, or to extreme volume, seen in the deep billowing frill of Balenciaga's cape-like jacket and the enveloping folds of Céline's cocoon coat. Designers such as Junya Watanabe, with his puffa dress, merely inflate the silhouette, whereas design duo Viktor & Rolf adapt the disciplines of topiary to create new forms. More extreme is the pumped-up volume of Thom Browne's fluorescent PVC jacket, featuring a sculpted six pack and perfect pecs. Although the designer is renowned for his shrunken, cropped version of the classic Brooks Brothers suit, he also plays with volume by referencing Herman Munster in a cartoon-like preppy blazer.

Throughout the evolution of fashion, numerous designers have played with the notion of distortion and directly confronted the idea of fit and its relation to the form of the body. In the 1990s, Issey Miyake took liberties with the silhouette and changed the natural form of the body by subordinating shape in favour of the active characteristics of innovative textiles. The following decade, Junya Watanabe for Comme des Garçons added a fold-down portable ruff to a minimal panné velvet sheath dress, elevating a simple garment to extraordinary status by the addition of an outsize accessory. Distortion can also be effected by a play on surfaces, most particularly the visual conundrum created by optical illusion, seen in Jean Paul Gaultier's Op art jumpsuit.

There are no fixed elements to the one hundred designs in *Why You Can Go Out Dressed Like That*. The garments do not have to fulfil a function, keep the wearer warm or increase sexual attraction, nor do they have to beguile or disarm. Their purpose is to show that there are no limits to the creative imagination in clothing the human form.

GUIDE TO SYMBOLS

 Explains why the design is important in the creative development of fashion.

 Describes the designer's approach, process and technique.

 Locates the design in its historic and fashion context.

 Unattributed quotes are by the designer featured.

 Provides additional incidental information.

 Lists examples of similar garments and their designers.

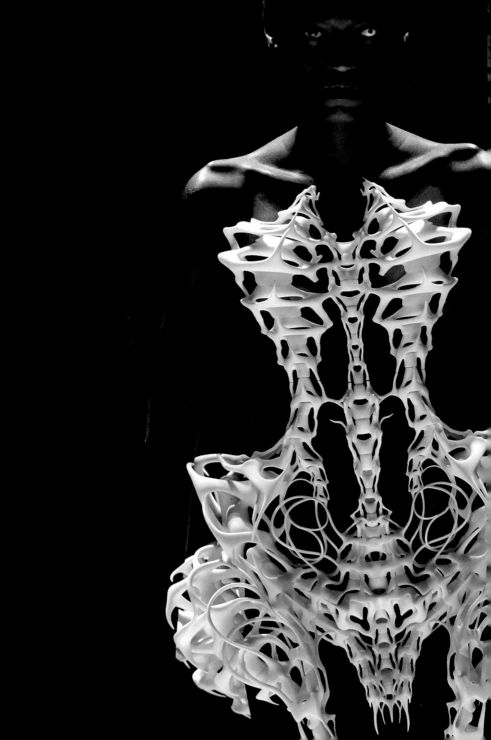

CHAPTER ONE
FANTASY

Fuelling a fantasy is about attaining the unattainable. Fantasy fashion not only embraces the light-hearted, as seen in John Galliano's two-dimensional paper-doll dress and Meadham Kirchhoff's princess bride, but also it can have a darker, more gothic edge. Edgar Allan Poe's narrative poem 'The Raven' (1845) inspired Alexander McQueen to create a brooding masterpiece. Constructed from deep-dyed feathers, it is a walking facsimile of the bird of ill omen. Fantasy fashion can be as simple as appearing as an animated pom-pom in Sister by Sibling's all-white coat, or more complex, such as the elaborate arrangement of references seen in Thom Browne's Red Queen dress.

A master of self-promotion, Poiret used novel methods to introduce his designs to a wide clientele. In 1908, he commissioned artist Paul Iribe to illustrate a bound album of his creations, *Les robes de Paul Poiret*—a radical departure from the existing tradition of fashion illustration—to be circulated among potential clients. A few years later, in 1911, Poiret held 'The Thousand and Second Night' party, a lavish ball in which Ottoman-influenced costumes were provided for any of the 300 guests who attended unsuitably attired.

In 1911, Poiret founded Ecole Martine, where disadvantaged girls were taught the decorative arts.

Gowns that Express Poetic Ideas, 1913
Lucile (Lady Duff-Gordon)

Leopard print lampshade dress, S/S 2007
Chanel

Strapless evening gown, 2007
Marchesa

LAMPSHADE DRESS
POIRET
1913

At the beginning of the 20th century, Paul Poiret (1879–1944) directly opposed the rigidity of the prevailing 'S'-shape corset and the matronly curves of the belle époque with costumes that evoked the Near, Middle and Far East. His designs included the introduction of the Directoire silhouette in 1906, a revisiting of the columnar shape popular during the French Directory period (1795–99), which was, in turn, modelled on ancient Greek dress. Launched in 1913, the 'lampshade' dress—worn by French actress Cora Laparcerie—is lightly gathered from a horizontal band above the breasts and caught in at the high waist with a matching band of embroidered fabric. The overskirt is wired at the base to provide a rigid circular hem, which is edged with a deep lampshade fringe. This is worn over diaphanous harem trousers, in lavishly embroidered silk, gathered at the ankle. In a further pastiche of Ottoman court costume, an aigrette is perched on the turban. The aigrette originally consisted of the head plumes of the egret bird and, when worn by the sultan, the headdress was studded with diamonds and rubies. The 'Arabian' slippers curl upwards and inwards at the toe, and festoons of pearl necklaces cascade around the head and body.

After working for Jacques Doucet and the House of Worth, Poiret opened his own couture house on rue Auber in Paris in 1903. His revolutionary approach to dressmaking and his interpretation of exoticism secured him international recognition until after World War I, when the modernity of the streamlined chemise replaced Poiret's complex embellishment. The house closed in 1929.

Poiret was one of the first couturiers to disseminate to a wider audience the dazzling colours and exuberant embellishment of Léon Bakst's costume designs for the Ballets Russes, launched in Paris in 1909. He also introduced the bifurcation of women's dress with Persian-inspired *jupes-culottes* in 1911, one of the first examples of trousers for women outside of Amelia Bloomer's practical cycling bloomers.

Despite regulation L85, announced in 1942 by the US War Production Board, which limited the amount and type of permissible clothing materials and decreed that the silhouette remain unchanged, the singer's multipatterned sarongs and ruffled boleros could be made easily by the home dressmaker and tapped into the growing US trend for resort wear. Carmen Miranda also popularized costume jewelry, which was large and theatrical and made no attempt to imitate precious jewelry.

CARNIVAL STYLE CARMEN MIRANDA 1941

Known as 'the lady in the tutti-frutti hat' after her appearance in the Busby Berkeley musical *The Gang's All Here* (1943), Carmen Miranda became the most popular entertainer in the United States in the 1940s by successfully adapting Bahian style and the Brazilian samba for a wider audience. Only 1.5 metres (5 ft) tall, the singer created her indelible image of fruit- and flower-festooned headdresses and towering sequinned platform-soled shoes to create greater impact on stage and screen. Her appearances also included a lavish application of outsize costume jewelry, then at the height of its popularity. In the late 1930s, Art Deco was reworked into a dramatic style of abstract and geometric shapes, seen here in the square pendant set with large, semi-precious stones that the actress donned in *That Night in Rio* (1941). It is worn alongside tetrahedron-shaped baubles and strands of beads, as well as beaded bracelets and earrings formed from clusters of multicoloured glass flowers. Wartime exigencies included tucking the hair into a turban for factory work, and Carmen Miranda glamorized the style by using gold lamé and adding height with fabric flowers with curled stamens projecting outwards. The midriff-baring, off-the-shoulder blouse with voluminous puffed sleeves has single paillettes tucked here and there among the folds. The high-waisted skirt with geometric patterning emphasizes the singer's tiny waist.

With her Latin rhythms and flamboyant costumes, Carmen Miranda provided a welcome distraction from wartime austerity. Her outfits were made using materials that replaced those rationed by the government, such as leather, wool, straw and raffia, with cork and wood used for the platforms of her shoes. Many of these were designed by Ted Saval of California, who produced a less extreme version for her followers. The elevated sole, with the toe lower than the heel and without a distinctive heel, formed the wedge shoe, which was popularized further by Italian shoemaker Salvatore Ferragamo.

Bettina blouse, 1952
Givenchy

Puffed sleeve dress,
S/S 2008
Christian Lacroix

Carmen Miranda was born Maria do Carmo Miranda da Cunha in 1909. She first appeared on Broadway in 1939 and within five years she had become the highest-paid actress in Hollywood. She symbolized not only Brazil but also South American Latino style.

Look at me and tell me if I don't have Brazil in every curve of my body.

One of the most enduring status symbols in 1960s fashion is a dress of silk jersey with the signature 'Emilio' worked into the border of the polychromatic abstract print. Pucci recognized the need for high-end, lightweight, travel-friendly leisurewear when jet aircraft went into wide-scale commercial service in 1960, bringing the leisured 'beautiful people' to the playground shores of the Italian coast. The designer introduced stretch into fabrics with 'Emilioform', an elasticized silk shantung that showcased his distinctive engineered prints, and Capri pants, a cropped narrow-legged trouser that has become a fashion staple.

**KAFTAN
PUCCI
1967**

Designed by renowned 20th-century print maestro Emilio Pucci (1914–92), the kaftan is worn by model Simone D'Aillencourt inside Lake Palace in Udaipur, India, a favoured destination in the 1960s of the newly mobile jet set, which included style icon Jacqueline Kennedy. Preferred garb of the counterculture that sourced the vernacular garment on the hippy trail to India, the kaftan was appropriated by designers and reimagined in luxurious fabrics and embellishment. The transparent silk chiffon, with a psychedelia-inspired print in fuchsia, red, pistachio green, aqua and yellow, is fashioned into a simply constructed 'T' shape: the sleeves are cut in one with the body of the garment and slashed at the neck, utilizing the width of the fabric. Each colour of the print required a separate silk screen, thus allowing no overlapping or overprinting of colour and resulting in the clarity and definition of the distinctive design. The kaftan is partnered with a pair of solid-colour, loose, wide-legged trousers with a narrow decorated hem. The full maquillage, lavish jewelry and high-piled hair distance the Pucci kaftan from its more informal counterpart.

Blue silk kaftan, 1965
Bill Blass

Yellow print kaftan, 1969
Zandra Rhodes

Chiffon print kaftan, 1969
Ossie Clark

In 1947, Pucci set up an haute couture house in the fashionable resort of Canzone del Mare on Capri, later moving to Rome and establishing headquarters in Florence. He was honoured with a special award from the Council of Fashion Designers of America in 1990. The brand suffered from the introduction of mass-produced copies and lost authority during the minimalistic 1990s, but the renewed popularity of print in the 21st century has seen the label revive under the direction of Pucci's daughter, Laudomia.

Vernacular garments from the hippy trail to India and the Far East, including variations of the 'T'-shape kaftan, appeared as high-fashion garments in the collections of leading European and US designers such as Thea Porter, Zandra Rhodes and Bill Gibb during the 1960s. The printed kaftan continues to have overtones of a hippy, laid-back lifestyle and remains a resort favourite, produced by contemporary designers such as Allegra Hicks and Matthew Williamson.

I enjoy much more designing informal clothes where the imagination is set free.

EMILIO PUCCI

The experimental fashion of Rabanne, alongside fellow designers of futuristic fashion André Courrèges and Pierre Cardin, was adopted by mass-market manufacturers using inferior fabrics. Chain mail was difficult to replicate, and its weight and rigidity rendered it impractical for daily wear. However, Rabanne achieved commercial success with chain-mail accessories, such as belts and his cult chain-mail bags. Modern techniques of textile development are capable of producing similar effects to chain mail without the drawbacks of inflexibility and volume.

Moon Girl collection, 1964
André Courrèges

Metallic foil dress, 1966
Betsey Johnson

Dress with silver hardware and cut-outs, 1968
Pierre Cardin

**CHAIN-LINK DRESS
PACO RABANNE
1969**

Spanish-born Francisco Rabaneda y Cuervo (1934–), known as Paco Rabanne, eschewed traditional techniques and dressmaking processes to produce his signature chain-link dresses that were futuristic in style and yet resonant of medieval armour. In this example, the medieval warrior transmutes into an impermeable 1960s chick, with a streamlined shimmer of an abbreviated tabard, or habergeon. The apron front is constructed from a metallic knitted mesh and worn over a skirt of overlaid metal discs. The chain links on the front panel of the tabard are attached to the fabric beneath, leaving the side panels bare for ease of movement. As with armour, the metal sleeves are not inserted into the arm scye but attached only at the sleeve head and allowed to fall into a wide, trumpet shape. The tabard is secured with a broad chain-link belt that is fastened with a circle of raised discs. The chain-mail hood extends into a hauberk, armour for the neck, below which three-dimensional metal discs are joined to form a camail, or mail collar. Further acknowledgement of medieval armour is seen in the flourishes of marabou feathers on the metal coif and woven into the mesh of the sleeves, where they are interspersed with rectangles of Rhodoid.

An eager exponent of new materials and techniques, fashion iconoclast Rabanne brought his experience of industrial design to his first 'body jewelry' collection of dresses in 1966. Constructed using metal cutters, pliers and a blowtorch, rather than a sewing machine and thread, the collection was a provocative manifesto titled 'Twelve Unwearable Dresses in Contemporary Materials'. The designer experimented with squares and discs of Rhodoid—a cellulose acetate—hammered metal, knitted fur, aluminium jersey and fluorescent leather and glass fibre. Rabanne patented the Giffo process in 1968, in which all the component parts of garments, including the buttons and pockets, were moulded in one piece.

Fashion, product design and interiors were enlivened by futuristic influences during the 1960s, prompted by the Space Race and the first moon landing. The streamlined styles heralded a period that looked forward to infinite progress and a future free of constraints, particularly sexual inhibitions, epitomized by Rabanne's costumes for Jane Fonda in Roger Vadim's sci-fi sex romp *Barbarella* (1968).

The woman of tomorrow will be efficacious, seductive and without contest superior to man. It is for this woman that I conceive my designs.

One rhinestone is never enough when two or six hundred will do. Mackie's approach to dressing performers is one of high-octane glamour and virtual undress, a style that is well suited to the Las Vegas Strip-based burlesque shows *Hallelujah Hollywood* (1974–80) and *Jubilee!* (1981–), for which he designed the costumes. His slashed, tasselled, feathered and frilled thigh-grazing dresses, beaded bra tops, sweeping capes and shiny stretch pants can also be seen on a range of collectable Barbie dolls, including Brazilian Banana Bonanza Barbie.

Cheryl Cole's dress, 2009
Julien Macdonald

Knitted dress, 2011
Mark Fast

SHOWGIRL
BOB MACKIE
1986

Introduced by actress Jane Fonda with the words, 'Wait'll you see what's gonna come out here,' Cher emerged on to the stage at the Academy Awards ceremony in 1986 wearing a showstopping nearly there outfit by the quintessential celebrity designer Robert Gordon 'Bob' Mackie (1940–). It was inspired by the lavish costumes designed by Erté, the leading exponent of extravagant theatricality for the *Ziegfeld Follies,* a series of revues on Broadway, and with it Mackie created a female archetype: the celebrity showgirl. His combination of the black strapping of the dominatrix with burlesque feathers and tassels makes this one of the most memorable Oscar outfits of all time. The serrated edge of the skirt, poised perilously just below the hip bone, is matched to the points of the bra top. Diamonds are placed discreetly over the nipples, and rhinestone-encrusted latticework extends to the high neckline, each section studded with gems. The towering Mohican headdress, sprouting black plumes one-and-a-half-times the height of Cher's head, is held in place with a zigzag rhinestone headband. Black stretch pants provide a novel opacity, worn beneath a bejewelled loincloth and with pointed high-heeled boots. A silk-satin rhinestone-studded cape draped over one shoulder adds a note of flying wonder woman.

> *Those crazy outfits for Cher weren't fashion, just goofy get-ups that were fun or stylish in their way.*

Mackie first worked as a sketch artist for legendary costumier Edith Head in 1961 while employed as a novice designer at Paramount Studios in California. A nine-times Emmy Award winner and Academy Award nominee, the designer is best known for his association with entertainment luminaries such as Judy Garland, Diana Ross and Liza Minnelli.

In the tradition of exhibitionism, the showgirl costume sits outside mainstream fashion: as an archetype of female glamour, certain components are required to remain the same. These include the feathered headdress, rhinestone-covered bra top and tailpiece. Since its inception in the 19th century, the costume has morphed into that worn by the surgically enhanced Las Vegas showgirl of today.

Sweet Lolita style occupies a curious place as both a breeding ground for new ideas and as a subculture to be mocked for its garish eccentricity. Japanese youth culture holds up a mirror to Western aesthetics, whether it is a Punk Lolita interpretation of Vivienne Westwood or a Ganguro girl's orange skin and bleached hair as a reflection of the Californian ideal. Street fashion photography has its origins in Tokyo, where posing in the latest customized ensemble is an integral part of a teenager's social life.

These garments, often handmade, are designed to define the wearer as a member of a particular tribe. The paradox within each subculture is the desire to blend in as a member of the tribe, by wearing matching outfits, while also wanting to stand out within the tribe by exaggerating key elements.

SWEET LOLITA
1990s

The four variations of the same outfit are typical examples of the Sweet Lolita style, one of the earliest and most familiar tribes of Japanese street style. The outfits appropriate a sense of Victorian gothic but are given a saccharine twist with the use of infantile design motifs, pastel colours and whimsical accessories. In each case, a wire-hooped petticoat acts as the foundation of the garment, creating a short, baby-doll pinafore dress in the style of a Victorian doll. The overdress consists of either white or black fabric printed with a series of nursery images, including a rocking horse and lollipops. A prim blouse of pink satin is worn under each dress, with capped sleeves and a collar trimmed with pink lace. The brevity of the skirt is emphasized by the candy-striped tights in matching pastel colours. The impression of infantilism is enhanced by the pony- and heart-shaped handbags. Each outfit is completed with a tonally matching wig and headpiece: the hair a more vibrant shade of pink than that seen in the dresses, topped with an oversized bow. Traces of the geisha tradition are seen in the mask-like pale faces and immaculate eye make-up, which also convey a doll-like passivity of expression.

Red pinafore dress,
S/S 2012
Meadham
Kirchhoff

Gothic Lolita,
S/S 2013
Anna Sui

The cerebral aestheticism of Japan's high-fashion conceptualists, such as Rei Kawakubo and Yohji Yamamoto, stands in stark contrast to the exhibitionism of the street styles of Japan's youth subcultures, in which teenage girls consume a variety of exaggerated looks in pursuit of belonging to a defined subgroup.

As well as designing staple garments such as the pinstripe suit, tuxedo, blazer and safari suit for both men and women in a radical shift in gendered dressing, the designer also brought to the couture runway a level of workmanship that elevated the garments to museum-quality works of art. His passion for theatre design—Saint Laurent's first of many stage and film costumes was designed for Roland Petit's ballet company in 1959—often translated into theatrical runway shows, best exemplified by the influential 'Opéra Les Ballets Russes' collection of 1976, which was internationally acclaimed as his most beautiful.

FEATHERED CAPE
YVES SAINT LAURENT
1990

Yves Saint Laurent (1936–2008) not only expressed his love of the exotic through the use of lavish embellishment and a vivid palette but also in his appropriation of natural found materials, such as feathers, wood and raffia. Saint Laurent had previously used feathers in 1969 for a collection of evening dresses made entirely of bird of paradise feathers, and his adroitness with the material is exemplified here in a cape that consists of ostrich and ring-necked pheasant tail feathers in tawny brown, deep red and black. It is a garment that evokes power rather than femininity, particularly in movement, and it is recognizably associated with the feather capes, known as *kahu huruhuru*, worn by Maori chieftains to indicate high rank. Each feather of the full-length cape was individually hand-stitched to the base material by the House of Lemarié, an atelier, now owned by Chanel, that has supplied feathers to the couture houses since it was founded in 1880. Accessorized with a wide copper cuff, chandelier earrings and a feather-shaped hair ornament, the model shows off the dramatic potential of the feathered cloak with her kinetic pose.

Ostrich-feather evening gown,
1928
Louiseboulanger

Ostrich-feather evening gown,
1933–35
Gabrielle 'Coco' Chanel

Feathered evening gown, 1968
Hubert de Givenchy

In 1983, Saint Laurent was featured in a twenty-five-year retrospective exhibition of his work at the Metropolitan Museum of Art in New York, the largest show ever given to a living couturier. Having consolidated his position as the most celebrated and revered designer of the late 20th century, he delegated the responsibility for his men's and women's ready-to-wear lines to Hedi Slimane and Alber Elbaz, respectively, in order to concentrate solely on the haute couture collections.

? Traditionally, feathers have been used in fashion to signify male supremacy or feminine coquettishness, and they are usually used as trimmings. The time-consuming process of creating an entire garment in feathers—split, dyed, twisted and individually attached to a base fabric—is one that can be undertaken only by haute couture. Fake feathers often replicate the effect of real feathers, as seen in Sarah Burton's ice-queen gown for Alexander McQueen in 2011.

I am naive enough to believe that [my designs] can stand up to the attacks of time and hold their place in the world today.

Divine in Pink Flamingos, 1972 directed by John Waters

RuPaul, 1992 Thierry Mugler

With his propensity to change his identity and remake his physical appearance, Bowery set the paradigm for outrageous fashion and validated the cult of the individual, recognizing no boundaries in either behaviour or appearance. He presided over a generation of designers, including Vivienne Westwood, John Galliano and Alexander McQueen, and evidence of his influence can still be detected in the unbridled exuberance of contemporary designers such as Meadham Kirchhoff and Walter Van Beirendonck and performers such as Lady Gaga.

BABY-DOLL DRESS
LEIGH BOWERY
1994

Club promoter, designer and long-time model for artist Lucien Freud, Leigh Bowery (1961–94) was a leading figure in London's style-fixated underground scene in the mid 1980s. A self-created living sculpture, Bowery transformed his body by moulding and taping his torso, adorning his distorted silhouette with a series of perverse and outrageous costumes, which he wore to the nightclub Taboo, London's version of Studio 54 in New York. In the baby-doll dress, his large frame is shoehorned into a bra-shaped top of leaf-green silk-satin, the shallow revers of the bodice turned over in a crumb-catcher collar. The exposed décolletage is filled in with a flesh-coloured turtle-neck sweater. A flourish of ostrich feathers appears at each wrist, and more feathers make up the baby-doll skirt in a travesty of frou-frou femininity. This ends at crotch height to display black-clad legs balanced on towering platform shoes. Bowery's heavy maquillage beneath the melted wax dripping down his bald pate is a grotesque parody of glamour: eyes encircled in green shadow and an oversized mouth drawn in red lipstick. Heavily rouged cheeks do not disguise the holes that he pierced for the insertion of safety pins, with which he would attach fake smiling lips to his face.

After the demise of Taboo, Bowery diverted his energies in the latter part of the 1980s to staging live performances, one of which involved 'giving birth' to his friend and wife, Nicola Bateman. During the performance, she hung upside-down beneath Bowery's extended belly before emerging covered in 'blood', lubricant and strings of sausages. In 1988, the Anthony d'Offay Gallery in London invited Bowery to stage an installation in which he sat behind a two-way mirror in a variety of costumes and wigs. It was at this time that he came to the attention of Lucien Freud, Britain's leading figurative painter. Freud's series of nude portraits (1990–95) are Bowery's lasting legacy.

In his pathological exhibitionism, Bowery used his body, and the extraordinary costumes that he created for himself, to construct an identity. This occurred in tandem with the New Romantic movement, a post-punk street style dominated by the pirating of ideas, sexual ambiguity and competitive narcissism, epitomized by the bands of the era, such as Duran Duran and Boy George's Culture Club.

Leigh was certainly not vain, but he was excessive in his self-exposure.

CERITH WYN EVANS, SCULPTOR AND FILMMAKER

Immaculate tailoring, heritage fabrics such as tweed and the implication of sporting prowess all go to make equestrian-inspired clothing uniquely attractive to the non-rider. By wearing some aspect of the uniform, urbanites can be associated with the elite activity of horsemanship and all it entails. Conversely, the leather strapping and severity of cut may be subverted to imply the accoutrements of the dominatrix.

EQUESTRIAN OUTFIT

DIOR

2000

Taking an equestrian-inspired look to extremes, John Galliano (1960–) for Dior dresses up the model to resemble a horse, complete with a long flowing tail extruding from the handbag, which forms the saddle. Other accoutrements of horsemanship appear elsewhere in the autumn/winter collection in more subtle form: second-skin denim is worked into hot pants bound with a broad leather belt at the hips, held together with a pair of stirrup-shaped buckles, and wrap-over leather skirts have a yoke shaped like a saddle, from which the webbing girth straps are allowed to fall free. Galliano's preoccupation with 18th-century tailoring is also given an airing in tan leather trousers with a button-down flap and a military-cut jacket, double-breasted and cropped at the waist. Here, the grey frock coat is cut with a series of diagonal seams from the arm scye and side seam to the centre front, creating fullness at the hem that then falls away in fluted panels to the back of the knee. The collar is cut to stand away from the neck, the wide revers extending to the narrow sleeve head. Horse's ears are attached to the rider's hard hat, and the incongruous geisha visage, half-moon glasses and off-centre, roughly applied lipstick provide an unlikely adjunct.

Since the phenomenon of the 'It' bag, the catwalk is often used as a vehicle to showcase the latest bag designs. By incorporating design elements of the Dior saddle bag into the catwalk collection, Galliano was promoting the desirability of the bag and endowing it with 'must-have' status. Accessories are vital to upholding the financial success of a label, and provide a more affordable way of buying into the brand. The accessory is identified easily by the initial 'D' dangling from each saddle-shaped bag.

Leather riding habit, S/S 2011
Jean Paul Gaultier

Harness dress, A/W 2012/13
Hervé Léger

Responsible for the regeneration of couture after the austerity of World War II, Christian Dior introduced the influential Corolle line in 1947, which heralded a newfound elegance and luxury that made him a household name. In 1996, London-based designer Galliano was appointed as creative head of the House of Dior, where he effected his own aesthetic of romantic fantasy until his summary dismissal in 2011.

I'm a romantic, I love superb craftsmanship, tailoring. . .I would say they are the codes of what represents John Galliano.

JOHN GALLIANO

Fashion fantasist Galliano deployed an eclectic bricolage of influences. These included a limitless cultural omnivorousness that ranged across the globe. He also referenced styles and sensibilities from the past, such as the wide-skirted, 18th-century *robe à la française*. The designer was a master of the bias-cut, redefining the 1930s-inflected line for a contemporary audience. Galliano's fashion house celebrated its twenty-fifth anniversary in 2009, since when he has been ejected from the company by its board.

By 2008, Galliano was designing nineteen collections a year, for Dior and his own label.

Miniature dolls in handmade dresses, 1996
Viktor & Rolf

Polka-dot dress, S/S 2008
Betsey Johnson

Fuchsia-pink chiffon pinafore, 2011
Meadham Kirchhoff

PAPER-DOLL DRESS
JOHN GALLIANO
2000

John Galliano (1960–) tapped into every young girl's fantasy of dressing cardboard dolls with two-dimensional paper cut-outs when he presented a living, walking, life-size doll on the catwalk. The flat silhouette is held in place by the model, and the broken line of the tabs, indicating the potential fold used to hold a paper dress in place on a doll, is left here to extrude beyond the outline. In an uncomfortable juxtaposition, the Lolita-type figure wears a boned corselet, named a 'Merry Widow' after the 1905 opera by Franz Lehár. This is edged with a static frill and worn over an abbreviated flounced baby-doll skirt to which two suspenders are attached. The two-dimensional garment is anchored by narrow spaghetti straps and worn over brief knickers, just visible beneath the hem of the tutu. A matching two-dimensional tiara with drawn-in gems is perched askew on an abundance of golden ringlets and a crudely cut fringe. Numbered areas recall the 'colour by numbers' activity that children enjoy, and the skirt is unfinished with a child-like scrawl of pale pink paint across the white background. Thighs and face are likewise imprinted with arbitrary splashes of iridescent paint in pale blue, the pastel tones enhancing the girlishness of the image.

Galliano consistently offers a more playful and irreverent aesthetic for his own label in contrast to his reverence for the codes of heritage fashion house Dior, for which he produced both ready-to-wear and couture collections. Here, he infantilizes his models by casting them as little girls let loose with their mothers' wardrobes or conversely as animated dolls, a variant on the inanimate mannequin.

From his French Revolution-themed graduation collection in 1984 to his first couture show for Dior in January 1997, Galliano set the paradigm for spectacle that also told a story. Sometimes accused of romantic excess and self-indulgent theatricality at the expense of wearability, the designer nevertheless combines an other-worldly glimpse of the fantastic with an astute commercial eye.

A garment of striking idiosyncrasy, the swan dress invited inevitable parodies: by Ellen DeGeneres at the Emmy Awards in 2001 and by Kevin James, who wore a version of it at the People's Choice Awards in 2002. The outfit has stayed in the popular consciousness far longer than more traditional occasion-led ensembles, leaving many pundits to regret the influence of the stylists who now dominate the red carpet.

OSTRICH DRESS
MARJAN PEJOSKI
2001

Macedonian-born, London-based designer Marjan Pejoski (1968–) is unlikely to escape the notoriety that has resulted from his design work for Icelandic artist Björk. The singer wore the infamous swan costume to the 73rd Academy Awards ceremony in 2001, and it came to be seen as one of the most absurd red-carpet dresses of all time. The absurdity was reinforced when Björk theatrically mimed laying an egg on the carpet, and the outfit was received with scathing vitriol by the fashion press. The performer later wore the ensemble for the cover photograph for her album *Vespertine* (2001) and also appeared in variations of the dress for her 'Vespertine' tour. Here, Björk's all-white swan is reiterated—as an ostrich—in black tulle, with the head of the bird rearing upwards rather than winding around the singer's neck and modestly resting its head and beak on her breasts. In classical literature, the swan's neck is perceived as a phallic symbol; in Greek mythology Zeus loved Leda and seduced her by transforming himself into a swan. The allusive sexual imagery is both consolidated and confused by the bare breasts of the model. Strangely configured tights attempt to replicate the legs of the ostrich, ending in a three-toed foot at the ankle.

Eschewing everyday staples for the opportunity to showcase idiosyncratic ideas—a fluted skirt with an appliquéd padded horse galloping across the yoke, bunches of grapes hanging from a vine and a dress made of faux peacock feathers—the designer frequently introduces three-dimensional decoration into his clothes. Having achieved cult status for his diverse and outré output, Pejoski now shows in Paris.

Red swan headpiece and wedding dress, S/S 2012
Giles

Feather and tulle wedding dress, A/W 2012/13
Chanel

Swan Lake wedding dress, 2012
Vivienne Westwood

Having moved to London in 1989, Pejoski studied jewelry, shoe design and fashion illustration before graduating from Central Saint Martins College of Arts and Design in 1999, the same year that he began his association with Björk. He launched his eponymous label in 2000, adding menswear in 2003. Pejoski is also the creative director of the label KTZ, a collaboration between himself and Sasko Bezovski.

Bezovski and Pejoski co-founded the fashion and music retailer Kokon To Zai in 1996. With shops in Paris and London, the business also showcases and sometimes buys the graduate collections of emerging talents.

Lacroix made his mark on the international fashion press in 1987 when he introduced the pouf or puffball skirt, a radical departure from the prevailing power dressing of the decade, and was hailed as Paris's most lyrical designer. His debut show from his own couture house consolidated his reputation as the inheritor of Christian Dior's mantle, with a collection based on a lavish use of textiles, a return to the hourglass figure and an eclectic assortment of cultural references.

Wedding dress, S/S 2007
Jean Paul Gaultier

Wedding dress, A/W 2009/10
John Galliano

Haute Couture collection,
Spring 2013
Elie Saab

COUTURE WEDDING DRESS

CHRISTIAN LACROIX

2007

After a sensory overload of vibrant colour combinations and a juxtaposition of myriad contrasting textures and fabrics, Christian Lacroix (1951–) ended his autumn/winter 2007 show with a wedding dress of an almost subdued palette of gold, rose pink, scarlet and teal. Yet, the figure is less a bride and more a religious icon, rendered as a Madonna-like effigy and enveloped in rich, embellished folds of fabric. The medieval-inspired gown in gold figured brocade is softly gathered from a high waist, falling to the ankle in a bell shape, the surface overlaid with scallops of Chantilly lace. Lace is also appliquéd to the bodice, where the scallops form a gentle heart-shaped neckline. The traditional bride's train is substituted for an ankle-length cape falling from stiff pleats at the shoulders in a pale blue damask patterned with stylized sprigs and blossoms in gold, orange, turquoise and fuchsia. In keeping with the designer's propensity for theatrical Catholic imagery, Lacroix draws on the rites of Southern Europe and the promenades of the Madonna at saints' days and festivals for the headdress. An oversized crown of gilded foliage and flowers is studded with gems and balanced on a short tulle veil. The Lacroix signature embellishment, an ornate Maltese cross, is secured to the waist of the gown.

I just know that I like to give a touch of theatrical spirit in a flat world and era.

The Provençal roots of Lacroix—he was born in Arles, France—are evident in the designer's passion for vivid colours and decorative textiles with traditional and folk elements. With complex layers of trimmings, outsize costume jewelry, the incorporation of boning and lacing and the adoption of Catholic iconography, Lacroix defined a new level of theatrical luxury.

The traditional finale of an haute couture show is a wedding dress, a culmination of what has gone before on the catwalk that also encapsulates the aesthetic of the designer. Lacroix acknowledges the conventional requirements of full-length gown, veil and train, but imparts his singular vision in a lavish exposition of medieval and Catholic iconography. Bridal gowns are of vital importance to the commercial success of haute couture, utilizing the skilled embroidery and beading ateliers to the full.

Holland launched House of Holland in 2008, two years after the appearance of his 'fashion groupies' rhyming slogan T-shirts, which were emblazoned with irreverent text and were seen on the front row at London Fashion Week. The designer's youthful playfulness has also successfully translated into various collaborative projects, including 'H! by Henry Holland', a capsule collection for a British high-street store, and a range of hosiery. The label's e-commerce site was launched in 2013.

**EXTENDED KILT
HOUSE OF HOLLAND
2008**

British designer Henry Holland (1983–) offers a perky pastiche of Scottish baronial style in a collection that features tartan trews and mini kilts, as well as a faux coat of arms, in which the designer's long-term friend, model Agyness Deyn, is emblazoned on the shield. This coat of arms is used as an all-over print on a body-skimming catsuit and as a single motif on a calf-length grey jersey dress. Woven by Scottish heritage company Johnstons of Elgin, the purple and yellow 'House of Holland' tartan is configured into neat double-breasted jackets for both men and women. The men's jacket is cut along the lines of a Highland dress coat and is worn with matching trousers, with a flirty little half-kilt attached at the hip and kilt buckles at the ankle. Holland also plays with the proportions of the kilt, pulling it up underneath the arms and cropping it at the thigh; here, the full-length tiered tartan dress is cut straight across the breast, falling in fluted pleated layers to the ankles. Elsewhere, an overblown tartan is printed on to button-through shirt dresses and neat little shell tops. The Highland theme is extended to an across-the-body bag, designed by Katie Hillier, in the shape of a furry sporran and to tam-o'-shanters with tartan streamers and outsize pom-poms.

Tartan skirt, A/W 2012/13
Clements Ribeiro

Tartan coat, A/W 2012/13
Corrie Nielsen

Padded tartan duffel coat, A/W 2013/14
Moncler Gamme Bleu

Holland was awarded the 'Best Use of Tartan' prize at the Scottish Fashion Awards in 2008, and was one of the recipients of the British Fashion Council's Fashion Forward scholarship in 2012.

Astutely building the brand since the introduction of his slogan T-shirts in 2006, Holland reinforces his house motto, a 'Pash for Fash', with increasingly assured collections that nevertheless retain the label's signature irreverence. Designed for a youthful demographic, the label features an imaginative use of whimsical prints and an exuberant vibrant palette.

Tartan fabric consists of distinctive interlocking stripes running in both directions to form a check. It has its origins in the 3rd or 4th century, but reached its apotheosis in the 19th century with the tartan cult of the Scottish Highlands, inspired by the novels of Walter Scott. Initially used as a means to identify Scottish clans, tartan has consistently provided inspiration to a number of designers, including Vivienne Westwood. She associated it with punk and later used it for the tailored jackets and mini kilts of her 'Anglomania' collection of 1993.

At the end of the day, you have to just believe in your work because if you don't, it shows.
HENRY HOLLAND

Like other potent symbols such as the swastika, the cross cannot be separated from its connotations. It is the most recognizable symbol of Christianity and can never be perceived as secular. The use of the cross for adornment was initiated by the punk and goth fashions of the 1980s; since then, religious iconography has appeared in collections by designers such as Christian Lacroix and Dolce & Gabbana.

CRUCIFORM NECKLACE

ZIAD GHANEM

2009

In a collection of evening wear for both men and women, modelled by a cast of drag queens, singers and burlesque dancers of varying ages and sizes, London-based designer Ziad Ghanem consolidates his self-styled reputation as the 'cult couturier'. The variety show includes a dandy in a frock coat and jabot (ornamental frill), a bubble skirt with the words 'boy toy' appliquéd to the surface, asymmetrical Grecian draping and exquisitely beaded guipure lace fashioned into an hourglass corset. Together, the garments showcase a collection of couture-level construction and embellishment. The cross is a motif that is used throughout: small scale, it is tucked in among the layers of appliquéd guipure lace on the shoulders of a gown; large scale, it is attached to the front of a strapless cocktail dress in Valenciennes lace. In its extreme size, the padded and lace-covered crucifix is free floating, attached by a loop to the neck of a white silk organza blouse like an outsize necklace. It extends from neck to knee and is wider than the body of the fragile, androgynous male model. The flotsam of a negligee is many layered, with hand-rolled edges and cape-like sleeves, falling from a narrow Nehru collar to just below the hips.

With no formal fashion training, Lebanese-born Ghanem relocated in the late 1990s to London, where he started designing one-off pieces before launching his couture line in 2007. He also collaborated with the label Firetrap on a seven-piece capsule range—'The Immoralist'—comprising contoured denim pieces styled by celebrity stylist Alexis Knox. This was first shown under the designer's ready-to-wear label.

Byzantine cross on corset,
A/W 2012/13
Versace

Dress with Maltese Cross,
A/W 2013/14
Emilio Pucci

Ghanem's couture line is one of overstated glamour, created in luxuriously embellished fabrics and subverted by the use of transgender models and occasional idiosyncratic detailing. Eclectic and theatrical, the designer frequently introduces a highly corseted silhouette, constructed from high-gloss silk-satin, in tandem with a lavish use of lace and other luxury materials.

I am inspired by the beauty of the grotesque. I am gothic at heart, but at the same time camp and kitsch.

McQueen's approach to fashion combined the precision and traditions of tailoring with an unfettered but disciplined creativity. Never compromising on craftsmanship, the designer used innovative cutting and construction to serve his singular appreciation of the Romantic period, which began in Europe towards the end of the 18th century. The movement extolled the value of powerful emotion, such as horror, terror and awe, as a legitimate source of the aesthetic experience, especially when confronting untamed nature.

Peacock-feather dress,
1900–02
House of Worth

Feather dress, 2004
Chanel

DUCK-FEATHER DRESS
ALEXANDER McQUEEN
2009

Under the aegis of Alexander McQueen (1969–2010), feathers take on a deeply sinister edge rather than their more customary role as an accoutrement of the showgirl or the ultimate symbol of flighty femininity. From 'The Horn of Plenty' collection, the knee-length dress is constructed from thousands of duck feathers dyed black and intertwined to form a convincing, malevolent, brooding raven: a Romantic symbol of death. The garment also references 'The Raven' (1845), a narrative poem by Edgar Allan Poe, in which the raven is representative of 'mournful and never-ending remembrance'. McQueen imposes a bird-shaped silhouette; the nipped-in waist forms a long feathered neck, leading to a small round head, where the feathers form a point on the forehead. Adhering to a classic 1950s couture silhouette, the fullness of the bird's breast is sited on the model's hips, and the feathers sprout downwards and outwards to form a small fluted hem. The distorted sleeves, evidence of McQueen's customary emphasis on the shoulder, create folded wings, undulating from the neck. The designer presents a smooth shiny surface that reveals only the claw-like hands and the anonymous face of the model in a meticulously observed facsimile of a bird.

There's something kind of Edgar Allan Poe, kind of deep and kind of melancholic about my collections.

The feathered showpiece was constructed by *plumassiers*, or feather masters, in the workshops of the House of Lemarié, an atelier of the most highly skilled and specialized craftspeople in fashion. Lemarié has collaborated with many of haute couture's legendary figures, from Cristóbal Balenciaga to Yves Saint Laurent, and in 1996 the house was bought by Chanel, which remains its major client.

A leading protagonist of 20th- and 21st-century fashion design, McQueen was unrivalled in his presentation of mythic images, challenging existing perceptions while offering a unique point of view. Myths, dreams and fantasies are frequently explored by designers such as Walter Van Beirendonck, whose autumn/winter 1998/99 collection titled 'Believe' recalled a 19th-century fairy-tale phantasmagoria.

? Rather than aspiring to the notion of 'wearability', Meadham Kirchhoff reacts to the commerciality of fashion by developing ideas outside the mainstream. These are showcased in unconventional venues and situations, featuring cinematic Busby Berkeley-style tableaux or a series of opulent room sets. However, the spectacle is subsumed by the desirability of the pieces, which are delicately hand-wrought and technically perfect. The design duo demonstrates a sense of playfulness in the combination of saccharine sweet femininity and an eclectic range of historical references.

"

I think of the show like it's a concert. You need to give a performance and you need to give people your heart.

BENJAMIN KIRCHHOFF

**GOTHIC ROMANI
MEADHAM KIRCHHOFF
2010**

Meadham Kirchhoff subverts ideas of beauty and reacts against the stereotype of 'fashionability' by offering a complete princess-bride look in which full play has been given to the juxtaposition of colour, texture and embellishment. Trawling through the vast panoply of Romani culture, from India through to Spain, the design duo, Edward Meadham (1979–) and Benjamin Kirchhoff (1978–), combines neon colour with dressing-up box eclecticism and judicious quantities of tinsel and glitter. Each layer of the garment comprises a stand-alone piece of exquisite craftsmanship. Leavers lace is appliquéd to the fuchsia-pink silk-chiffon veil, edged with a serrated frill and topped with a Christmas cracker crown. A paler pink on grey is worked into a subtle silk-jacquard-brocade jacket, self-bound around the edges. The smock dress beneath, a marbleized print of amber on cream, falls to mid thigh and is worn over a polka-dot skirt, the exact shade of red to unite the orange and the pink. The edge of the full skirt is dagged in medieval style and trimmed with frills of lace, falling over a pair of practical slouchy socks and leather open-toed flat shoes. Arms stacked with glittering gold, silver and lamé bracelets and bangles accessorize the outfit and complete the psychedelic bride.

British designer Edward Meadham trained in womenswear and French-born Benjamin Kirchhoff took the menswear route. The Benjamin Kirchhoff label, a menswear line launched in 2002, was their first joint venture, but it was not until they showed in 2006 that they adopted the united branding for their womenswear label. At this time they introduced multitextured and polychrome body-sculpted minidresses, a foretaste of the multireferenced collections to come.

*Paisley, lace and satin dress,
A/W 2003/04*
Christian Lacroix

Wedding dress, S/S 2007
Jean Paul Gaultier

Deconstructed tutu, 2008
Rodarte

Meadham Kirchhoff's nonconformist aesthetic incorporates a romantic and sometimes perverse excess that invariably evolves from the development of various narratives. These diverse sources extend from the Rococo richness of the 18th century to Dario Argento's horror film *Suspiria* (1977) and the louche style of US singer-songwriter Courtney Love.

Meadham Kirchhoff designed a capsule collection of shredded chiffon and sequin-strewn dresses in a strict palette of nude and black for British high-street store Topshop for S/S 2010.

Against the grain of its signature aesthetic of razor-sharp tailoring linked to echoes of lingerie and corsetry, adopted by sultry movie muses Isabella Rossellini and Monica Bellucci in the 1990s, Dolce & Gabbana heralded the apotheosis of pop princess Kylie in a kitsch panoply of Olympian splendours.

APHRODITE: LES FOLIES
DOLCE & GABBANA
2011

Kylie Minogue's 'Aphrodite: Les Folies Tour' celebrated the Greek goddess of love, beauty and pleasure, while evoking the choreographed excess of the *Ziegfeld Follies* Broadway revues and the cinematic vision of Busby Berkeley films in the 1930s and 1940s. The tour was designed by Road Rage, comprising the singer's long-standing collaborator, director and stylist William Baker, and eight of the costume changes were outfits by Italian fashion house Dolce & Gabbana, founded by Domenico Dolce (1958–) and Stefano Gabbana (1962–). Playing with the notion of the Greek chiton, a garment originally made from two rectangles of cloth and worn loose, or gathered up by a girdle, the designers incorporate a gold leather stitched and boned metallic corset into the flowing silk-chiffon dress. This delineates the breasts and extends into a bra top, creating a ruched panel contained by ornate metallic shoulder straps. The skirt falls into gathers from a high waist, the front section tucked under to form a folded hem, in true chiton style. The skirt dips at the back to provide cascading folds of silk chiffon, interspersed with vertical rows of pearls, a symbol of fecundity. The Australian singer references the Greek god Hermes, messenger of the gods, with the winged helmet of stylized feathers and the rhinestone-studded knee-length gladiator sandals.

Riding the wave of high-voltage fashion, the house celebrates its version of the archetypal Sicilian temptress in lace, lingerie and leopard skin. The use of Catholic iconography adds a subversive edge to the overt sensuality of the label.

? Although extreme in its interpretation, Dolce & Gabbana is only one in a long list of design houses to refer to the draping and cutting of classical Greek dress in its contemporary fashion designs. Couturiers Mariano Fortuny, Madeleine Vionnet and Madame Grès reintroduced the simple, sculptural silhouette in the 1920s and 1930s, achieving the pliant and supple forms of the original. More recently, US designer Isabel Toledo has created ruched and pleated gowns in lightweight jersey and Greek-born designer Sophia Kokosalaki has introduced the draped folds seen in antique dress into her collections.

'*Blond Ambition Tour'*, 1990
Jean Paul Gaultier

'*I am. . .World Tour'*, 2009
Thierry Mugler

'*Diamonds World Tour'*, 2013
Adam Selman

**INSECT DRESS
BORA AKSU
2011**

> Fabric choice can make or break a garment therefore it needs so much personal consideration.

Turkish-born Bora Aksu first won Topshop NEWGEN sponsorship after graduating from Central Saint Martins College of Arts and Design in 2003, and immediately embarked on his own eponymous label. Aksu went on to win four consecutive NEWGEN sponsorships and he remains on the official London Fashion Week schedule. Notable collaborations include his work with film prop designers Artisan Armour in 2007, and brands such as Topshop, Nike, Converse and Anthropologie.

Reportedly inspired by watching a colony of ants one summer's afternoon, London-based designer Bora Aksu (1969–) presents models as giant perambulating versions of insects. Alongside a more relaxed silhouette of luminescent silver, paisley brocade, low-slung peg trousers and draped-sleeve blouses, the designer introduces structured ruffles, padded coils and piped fabric to convey the qualities of an ant. In a feat of clever construction around the corseted body, Aksu repositions the head, thorax and abdomen of the ant and superimposes the exoskeleton on the model's body, thereby creating a 1950s-inspired hourglass figure. In another designer's hands, the subject matter might result in a gothic horror, but Aksu's proficiency with drop-dead cocktail dresses has diffused the subject matter into a subtle glamour. The various parts of the insect are replicated in an intricate patchwork of effects and fabrics; draped folds of dark blue brocade are fashioned into a pannier-like overskirt, cut to display the flesh-pink silk-satin beneath. On either side of the centre front of the skirt, two smooth satin padded pieces create a heart shape, and layers of black silk chiffon over pink form the bodice. Tights in black and beige cut-out lace extend the theme, as do oversized ants nestling in the model's hair.

Black leather wingspan coat,
A/W 2012/13
Haider Ackermann

Beetle-printed dress,
A/W 2013/14
Lanvin

Combining contrasting fabrics with intricate inset cutting, and structured corseting with fluid layers, Aksu is a fashion romantic and the go-to designer for the modern cocktail dress, which he first presented in Paris in 2009. His craft-based aesthetic incorporates the traditional with couture techniques for a contemporary take on glamour.

Through his involvement with clothing label People Tree, founded by Safia Minney in 2005, Bora Aksu tries to incorporate as much ethically sourced material in his collections as possible.

Although myrmecophobia (fear of ants) is less common than arachnophobia (fear of spiders), the replication of any insect into wearable garb can cause disquiet. The reverse anthropomorphism of a human being given insect-like characteristics implies that the human takes on the qualities of the insect. This surreal transposition is not a frequent occurrence in mainstream fashion, and it is usually the provenance of the darkly gothic aesthetic of designers such as Rick Owens and Riccardo Tisci at Givenchy, where the webby intricacies of the spider are more common, particularly in knitwear. The carapace of the beetle is more frequently recognized in the rigid armature of designers who specialize in leather.

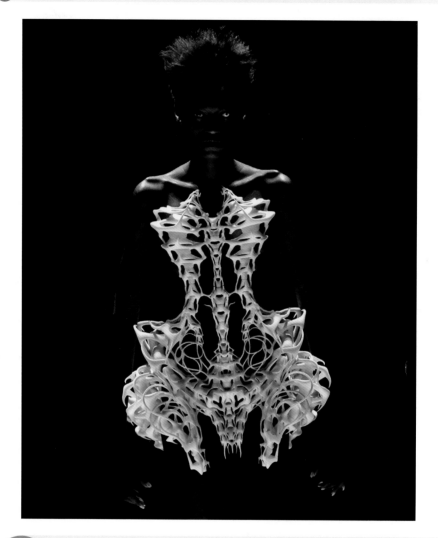

A pioneering designer, Van Herpen gives voice to the latent futurism of the 21st-century digital consumer. Through unbridled experimentation, she has conjured visions of the possibilities that second and third generations of 'new' technology provide—not for cheap production, but for richly enhanced, unprecedented artefacts that project a future golden age. This pioneering spirit is akin to the space-fiction futures embraced in the 1960s by designers such as André Courrèges and Pierre Cardin, who were inspired by the 'white-hot' technology of the Space Race.

SKELETON DRESS
IRIS VAN HERPEN
2011

Since the launch of her label in 2007, Paris-based designer Iris Van Herpen (1984–) has emerged swiftly into the limelight and into museum collections. The gothic technological modernism of her skeleton dress has established her three-dimensional printed and laser-cut assemblages as worthy of inclusion in any contemporary cabinet of fashion curiosities. This garment and other three-dimensional printed dresses are the fruit of Van Herpen's collaboration with the digital technology company Materialise and with architects Isaïe Bloch and Daniel Widrig. Underpinning the technological bravura, there is a distinct connection to the zoomorphic and biomimetic tendency in futuristic architecture, in which structural forms are transposed to the built environment from the organic patterns of growth in flora and fauna. The skeleton dress is created by a pulsed laser that layers powdered rubbers or metals into a shape calculated by a computer. These polymers craft a garment loosely derived from the internal scaffolding of fantasy vertebrates that approximate the human skeleton beneath. In other digital confections, Van Herpen uses stereolithography to create three-dimensional formed garments from liquid polymers that are hardened instantaneously by laser. This 'tech couture' may lead to a redefinition of what constitutes luxury high-end fashion.

Van Herpen is an advocate of the value of craft processes, including the highly nuanced exploitation of digital tools. Since the turn of the 21st century, crude 'rapid prototyping' equipment has evolved to the point of adoption for the manufacturing process itself. It is now seen as the new frontier of 'additive manufacturing', and direct printing from digital files into three-dimensional form in complex polymers and even metals can be achieved.

There's some futurism in what I do. . .but I'm really into old, forgotten crafts techniques, which I then combine with new materials and techniques.

Van Herpen has been empowered in her pursuit of extraordinary sculptural forms by the support of her collaborators, who share her enthusiasm for the adventure of radical creativity outside of consensus. For Materialise, the high-profile outcomes serve to publicize the technology developed by the company.

Three-dimensional printed gown for Dita von Teese, 2013
Michael Schmidt and Francis Bitonti

Black skeleton dress, 2013
Julia Koerner and Materialise

Van Beirendonck makes light work of the fragmentation of visual popular cultures, confidently repositioning the iconography and trappings of general apparel, dubious nightlife and irreverent graphics to spectacular effect. In strong catwalk collections, Van Beirendonck uses the impact of key hyperbolic outfits to confirm the span of his alchemical imagination, which is not invested in a single visual moment but in the transitions between the polar extremes of inspirational themes.

RUG COAT
WALTER VAN BEIRENDONCK
2011

In order to deliver a new visual narrative, Belgian designer Walter Van Beirendonck (1957–) avails himself of rich veins of cultural residue, bringing together a controlled fusion of disparate fragments and tastes.

An all-enveloping striped rag-rug mantle marks the apogee of escapism from any Eurocentric conformism. In this outfit, allusions to African mask dance costume are overt: from the styled coiffure to the layering of polychromatic fringing—shading from light brown to brightest turquoise—that forms a bulky knee-length cape, the connection to Dogon tribal mask dance dress is direct. Almost unseen, except at the hem of the cape, is the sartorial quirk of a slimline tailored suit, over which a narrow knee-length skirt is worn. The suit is intercut with appliqués of what might be Dutch–African wax prints in vibrant colours, an echo of the dandy elegance of the Brazzaville urban subculture of well-dressed gentlemen known as La Sape, or Société des Ambianceurs et des Personnes Élégantes. Van Beirendonck dares to shuffle elemental associations from the creation myths and the cosmology of Mali and Burkina Faso to the curious post-colonial appetite in the Republic of Congo for political dissent expressed through adaptations of dapper European tailoring.

Knitted cape, A/W 2011/12
Frankie Morello

Knitted cape, A/W 2011/12
Roberto Cavalli

Plaid tweed cape,
A/W 2011/12
Thom Browne

Van Beirendonck designs a children's collection, ZulupaPUWA, based on two of the designer's favourite tribes—the Zulus and Papuans—for Belgian fashion chain JBC.

From roots in the sober deconstructive ethos of 1980s Antwerp, Van Beirendonck's work has evolved to a form of cultural demolition, entwined with regeneration that puts humour and the radical at a premium. The experimental character of the collections is reinforced by the bold use of unusual and new materials in eccentric colour combinations.

? Although Van Beirendonck is exuberant and reckless in making jovial play with esoteric themes, he also offers sharply tailored suits in sartorially conventional hues—cream and grey—among the colourful and extreme ideas that constitute his collection. He has not only remained true to the brand values that originally placed him resolutely in the firmament of the avant-garde, but also has evolved into a high-profile publicist, producing catwalk extravaganzas that have given him credibility in music and theatrical design collaborations.

❝

It's not that I want to shock—that I'm searching for a shock value. I want to do something that people are questioning, or that they are surprised [by], so that they are seeing something.

Offering an exuberant and irrepressible take on classic knitwear, the Sister by Sibling label imbues the fashion staple with a sense of fun. The designers concentrate solely on knitwear—it is not an add-on to the main collection—so they are free to exploit the versatility of the genre. Technically adroit, they also produce more commercial pieces in which innovation overrides the showstoppers.

**POM-POM COAT
SISTER BY SIBLING
2013**

The second official season of the Sister label to be presented at London Fashion Week (the menswear label, Sibling, by the same designers launched in 2008) included Day-Glo colours of hot pink, chartreuse and lime green in homage to Poly Styrene, the British punk singer who died in 2011. Among the three-dimensional floral embellishment, toile de Jouy print dresses and skull intarsia cardigans of the 'Warrior in Woolworths' knitwear collection was a full-size pom-pom coat: a furry ball of lightweight frothy texture that brought to mind the rolling columns of a mechanical car wash. Knitted in white cotton on a coarse-gauge machine, the cardigan coat is completely enveloped in long white raffia tufting that has been hooked through the base fabric. A fully fashioned ribbed yoke extends to a grown-on neckline, which closes with a zip fastening at the centre front. Featured throughout the collection are babies' bonnets in pointelle lace stitch—most likely based on a 1950s hand-knit pattern for a baby's layette bonnet—with outsize Minnie Mouse ears made from added raffia pom-poms. Here, the bonnet is tied in a bow under the chin with a silk-satin ribbon, adding to the ingénue appeal. Vibrantly coloured shoes by British designer Sophia Webster add playful embellishment.

Cozette McCreery (1968–), Joe Bates (1967–) and Sid Bryan (1974–) of Sister by Sibling combine their playful exuberance with inventive techniques throughout their knitwear collections. In 2013, they designed a one-off dress, commissioned to celebrate the extended twentieth anniversary of Disneyland Paris. Inspired by Cinderella's ball gown, the costume was a knitted mini, featuring hand embroidery. The designers worked alongside Alber Elbaz of Lanvin, who redesigned Minnie Mouse's polka-dot frock on behalf of France.

Multicoloured pom-pom outfit, A/W 2009/10
Ashish

Pom-pom dress, 2013
BEINTAbeinta

With the infrastructure in place from the established Sibling label, the offshoot womenswear label, Sister by Sibling, was a natural next step for the design triumvirate. The three knitwear designers all act as consultants on a variety of other design projects, which results in a cohort of supportive connections, including the influential stylist Katie Grand.

There is a piece of joy in everything we do and that is the absolute lifeblood. As soon as you get that, you get us.
JOE BATES

The play on volume seen in Browne's womenswear is in marked contrast to the pared-down aesthetic of his menswear. The designer fails to acknowledge the female form without some element of distortion or cover-up, and he rarely exposes flesh. His only reference to the hourglass figure is to follow its parameters while extending its boundaries. Quantities of fabrics are deployed to this end—tailored, draped and gathered—often featuring signature checks and plaids.

RED QUEEN DRESS
THOM BROWNE
2013

New York-based designer Thom Browne (1965–) presents his version of Lewis Carroll's villainous character as a three-dimensional playing card, but he also includes all the physical characteristics of the Red Queen featured in Tim Burton's *Alice in Wonderland* (2010), from the red heart-shaped painted mouth to the towering upswept hair. Retaining the textured dogstooth checks more customarily used for his menswear collections, Browne builds a jacket and dress of surreal exaggeration. The strange proportion of the rectangular-shaped scarlet and white check jacket is outlined by a narrow black strip of fur along the outside of the shoulders and along the edge of the double-breasted fastening. The jacket is cropped at the waist, forming a horizontal line with the cape-like sleeves; it is cut to suppress movement and to create a sense of static theatricality. Beneath the jacket, a long-sleeved dress in dogstooth check flares to below the knee, where an inverted 'U' shape creates extra fullness at the hem. Scarlet Chantilly lace is appliquéd to the white silk chiffon of the high ruffled neck and cuffs of the blouse, a gothic sensibility that is repeated in the appliquéd red roses on thorny stems that twine around the white-clad legs. Demure lace-up shoes in grey are spattered with streaks of white paint.

Blue gingham Alice dress,
S/S 2010
Christopher Kane

Snow White outfit, S/S 2013
Meadham Kirchhoff

Michelle Obama wore a blue checked silk-jacquard Thom Browne coat dress for the Inauguration Day ceremonies after Barack Obama was sworn in for his second term as US President in 2013.

With no formal fashion training, Browne first worked as a salesman in Giorgio Armani's showroom in 1997, before heading the creative team at Club Monaco, a brand of the Polo Ralph Lauren Corporation. Browne launched his own bespoke suit label in 2001, adding his first women's pieces to the collection in 2007.

The absurd and the ridiculous hold an inherent attraction for the avant-garde fashion designer, and myths, fairy tales and fiction provide a rewarding source of both. In an editorial for US *Vogue* in 2003, photographed by Annie Leibovitz, 'Alice' appeared in a series of outfits by the world's most influential designers, alongside Viktor & Rolf as Tweedledum and Tweedledee and Stephen Jones as the Mad Hatter.

CHAPTER TWO
DISPLACEMENT

Displacement in fashion design provides the opportunity for designers to impose arbitrary, whimsical or inconsequential motifs, images or objects on to garments without reference to rationality, orderliness or logic. This allows for the introduction of perceived taboo materials, such as hair, blood and bone, into the design, as well as more light-hearted subject matter. Parisian couturier Emanuel Ungaro created an evening dress using ping-pong balls and Spanish designer Agatha Ruíz de la Prada combined a skirt with an upturned umbrella, complete with plastic raindrops. Two-dimensional images more usually seen on the walls of an art gallery are also displaced, such as Andy Warhol's *Campbell's Soup Cans* (1962) incorporated into the design of a disposable paper dress.

? Singularly well placed to exploit her artistic connections in Paris—her friends included Marcel Duchamp and Man Ray—Schiaparelli collaborated most successfully with Dalí. Offering a witty approach and elaborate visual jokes, her ideas were much copied, although at the time mainly in the area of accessories. It was not until the 1980s that Surrealism influenced mainstream fashion once again, exemplified by designers such as Franco Moschino and his teddy-bear coat and, more recently, by Martin Margiela and the avant-garde.

> *Two words have always been banned from my house—the word 'creation', which strikes me as the height of pretentiousness, and the word 'impossible'.*
>
> ELSA SCHIAPARELLI

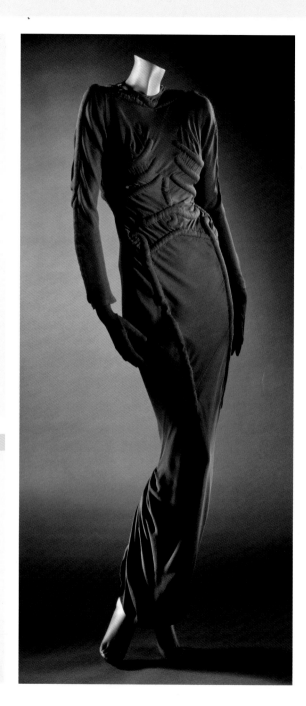

SKELETON DRESS
SCHIAPARELLI
1938

The use of taboo materials such as hair, blood, bone and skin in fashion has its provenance in Surrealism, a movement—founded by French writer and poet André Breton in the 1920s—that places the ordinary into a new, unsettling context. Italian couturière Elsa Schiaparelli (1890–1973) designed the skeleton dress with long-time collaborator Salvador Dalí, a painter of exquisitely executed dreamscapes of hypnagogic imagery. Shocking in its replication of the human skeleton, described in *trapunto* quilting on a fine matt black silk surface, the evening dress created outrage among Schiaparelli's peer group of designers. The 'bones' were stitched in outline through two layers of fabric, with cotton wadding inserted through the back to bring the design into relief on the front. The back of the garment is similarly inscribed: a ridged spine continues from the neck to just below the waist seam. Ever practical, Schiaparelli left the hip area clear for ease of sitting. The shoulder seams and right side are closed with bold plastic zips, which at the time were rarely used for garments and unseen on evening wear. The dress conforms to the prevailing silhouette of the period, with long, lean, body-skimming lines and a pronounced shoulder leading to a full-length, tight sleeve.

Schiaparelli launched her first collection in 1929 from rue de la Paix, Paris, comprising sportswear and ready-to-wear knitwear featuring trompe l'oeil effects, such as the best-selling bow-knot sweater. The designer opened one of the first couture boutiques, an offshoot of her couture house, at 21 Place Vendôme in 1935. Returning to Paris from New York after World War II, Schiaparelli curtailed her whimsical manner and gave way to the modern approach of her long-time rival Coco Chanel.

Catrina, A/W 2010/11
Givenchy

Skeleton dress for Nicki Minaj, 2010
Manish Arora

Skeleton dress, S/S 2011
Jean-Charles de Castelbajac

An iconoclastic designer, Schiaparelli incorporated her own idiosyncratic approach to fashion with experiments in textured fabric, working with Charles Colcombet, a French textile manufacturer. She focused on using the surface as a potential canvas for her surreal conceits, with the emphasis on design details and accoutrements fashioned into ephemera.

Schiaparelli introduced her scent Shocking in 1938. The shape of the bottle was based on the much-admired torso of one of her clients, Hollywood actress and sex symbol Mae West.

From knitted swimsuits, Gernreich branched out into knitted clothes, and then into a variety of fashions that the industry classified as sportswear, even though the designs included see-through chiffon dresses and shift dresses with vinyl cut-outs. He was one of the first designers to raise the hemline and the first to decorate the legs in patterned hosiery. He was awarded the Council of Fashion Designers of America Special Tribute in 1985.

I can't make a statement with a dress. It's the ring, the fingernail, the eye, everything.

HEAD-TO-TOE PRINT
RUDI GERNREICH
1966

Chief exponent of a 'total look', fashion maverick Rudi Gernreich (1922–85) collaborated with hosiery manufacturers and with footwear designers Capezio in order to emphasize the sense of a complete second-skin transformation. Here, he offers a Pop art version of animal prints in three patterned ensembles that clothe the body from head to toe, including the underwear. The small-scale black-and-white cheetah print is made up into a loosely belted shift dress, worn beneath a matching three-button blazer with rolled revers. A combined hat and snood is tucked into the neck of the dress, leaving only the upper part of the face exposed. Gloves, tights and shoes are fashioned in the same spotted pelt. The lustrous brown-and-black tiger-print ensemble is made up of exactly the same components. In contrast, the bold giraffe-print costume consists of a stencilled calfskin seven-eighths-length coat, worn with an above-the-knee skirt, printed turtle-neck top, with matching helmet and tights as well as shoes by Capezio. In order to introduce the notion of being totally coordinated from the skin outwards, the clothes were presented in a striptease. Revealing nothing but their eyes through the slits in their hoods, the models peeled off the layers, down to matching bra and tights.

Leopard-skin evening dress,
A/W 1997/98
Jean Paul Gaultier

Zebra-skin trouser suit,
S/S 2000
Roberto Cavalli

Leopard-print leather skirt,
A/W 2013/14
Burberry Prorsum

Having witnessed the avant-garde culture of interwar Vienna, Gernreich was propelled into radical fashion by spending time with the Lester Horton dance company, where he formulated many of his ideas about unrestrictive clothing. His designs were featured in what is regarded as the first fashion video, *Basic Black* (1967), directed by William Claxton.

Whether utilizing the original pelts or faux replicas, or reducing the pattern to an abstract form, fashion designers have long been fascinated by the power and effect of animal skins. A symbol of the predatory sex goddess throughout the 1950s, animal skins came to represent wayward female power. In contrast, by clothing the whole body from head to toe, Gernreich uses animal skins as a form of camouflage, in an attempt to appropriate some of the mythical qualities of the hunted beast.

Pop art has its roots in the late 1950s and was named when British artist Richard Hamilton and critic Lawrence Alloway defined the aesthetic challenge to Europe posed by US industrial culture. According to Hamilton, the new art should be 'popular, transient, low-cost, mass-produced, young, witty, sexy, gimmicky, glamorous, big business', all tenets that apply to The Souper Dress. The immediacy and accessibility of the screen-printing process enabled a speedy dissemination of Pop art style.

The first paper dress was created by the Scott Paper Company in 1966 as a marketing gimmick; the campaign was so successful that more than 500,000 dresses were sold.

Pop art sweater, 1971
Mike Ross

Checkerboard suit with Mao portraits, 1995
Vivienne Tam

Comic-book-text sweater, 2012
3.1 Phillip Lim

THE SOUPER DRESS
1966

The short, streamlined minidresses of the early 1960s, simple in design, easy to produce and with few construction details, provided a perfect canvas to showcase creative ideas, many of which were influenced by the artistic movements of the period. A screen-printed dress manufactured and sold by Campbell Soup Company in 1966, The Souper Dress was inspired by Andy Warhol's artwork titled *Campbell's Soup Cans* (1962). It epitomized the phrase 'planned obsolescence', coined by the US industrial designer Brooks Stevens in 1954, which described a culture in which the desire for the new replaced the virtues of longevity, and the paper dresses of the 1960s were termed 'throwaways'. Constructed from bonded cellulose fibre made into paper, the dress is simple in fit and construction. Two small darts lead from the bound cutaway armholes to the bust, creating the line of the skirt through the 'fit-and-flare' method, a popular device that provided the archetypal 1960s silhouette. The darts supply the only shaping; otherwise, the dress is sewn simply at the side and shoulder seams and features a boat-shaped neckline bound in black. The garment was not sold from a dress rail, but mailed flat to the buyer in an envelope. Although promoted as the ultimate in convenience, the disposable dress was a short-lived novelty item.

After the 'make-do-and-mend' ethos established as a result of post-war austerity, there was an explosion of newfound creativity in all the arts. During the 1960s, the eager consumerism of the era was exploited and disseminated through the fashion and art worlds in assemblages of cultural icons and found objects.

The Pop art movement removed the boundaries between high and low culture, elevating mundane imagery such as soup cans, comic books and advertisements to high-art status. These appeared on mass-manufactured garments by 'youthquake' designers of the time, including Betsey Johnson, and sold in New York boutiques such as Paraphernalia and in London. The flat, colourful images by practitioners such as Roy Lichtenstein and Richard Hamilton continue to be a persuasive presence in contemporary fashion, referenced by designers including Jeremy Scott and Henry Holland.

Ungaro rejected the traditions of couture by evolving a precision-cut and unadorned silhouette entirely in keeping with 1960s minimalism, shortening skirts to unprecedented lengths and exposing large amounts of flesh. The abbreviated, architectural line of the clothes is one that reappears consistently, and can be seen in the work of contemporary designers such as New York-based Louise Goldin.

**PING-PONG DRESS
UNGARO
1969**

One of the 1960s pioneers of the new French haute couture, alongside André Courrèges and Paco Rabanne, Italian-born Emanuel Ungaro (1933–) devoted his first collection of twenty pieces to daywear and refused to design evening wear, apart from one gown decorated with outsize ping-pong balls. This satirical gesture was the designer's protest against the haute couture industry's customary emphasis on formal dressing. The outfit is composed of a combination of guipure lace, a high-end fabric more usually confined to luxe evening wear, and white styrofoam, a low-end synthetic, used to create the ping-pong balls. The guipure lace cape is mid-calf length and flows from a circle of balls at the neck. Each floral motif of the lace features a suspended white styrofoam ball, which reportedly bounced and trembled with the model's movement. Matching cuffed shorts are gathered over the hips from a white metal yoke dipped at the front and shaped to the torso. The white metal bra top is moulded into two circular cones with a front fastening and a broad back strap, in a feat of engineering rather than dressmaking that was typical of the space-age futuristic fashion of the era. The model is styled with a towering edifice of hairpieces, with silver-hued plaits falling to the collarbone.

Ungaro worked two seasons with Courrèges, from 1964 to 1965, before establishing his own couture house with textile artist Sonja Knapp in 1965. His first collections followed the futuristic lines and abbreviated skirts of Courrèges but featured stronger, brighter colours, including vibrant pinks and oranges. Ungaro's predilection for colour was given full rein during the 1980s, with his vivid prints and befrilled, swagged and ruched evening wear.

It is part of the folklore of fashion that when a woman dresses for evening she changes composition—such nonsense.

EMANUEL UNGARO

Ungaro not only rejected the hierarchical and formal nature of couture, but was equally provocative in his presentation of the clothes and his choice of model. Black models were a rarity in the 1960s, and in 1966 Donyale Luna became the first African American model to appear on the cover of British *Vogue*.

Metallic foil dress, 1966
Betsey Johnson

Paillettes dress, 1966
Paco Rabanne

Iridescent metallic bikini, 1968
André Courrèges

During a career that lasted more than forty years, Saint Laurent created the paradigm of the contemporary wardrobe. He sidestepped Dior's mantle and produced fashion firsts that were influenced by the street: trousers for women, the pea jacket and the safari look. Aware of a youthful demographic that had no interest in couture, the designer opened his first prêt-à-porter boutique, Saint Laurent Rive Gauche, which both spearheaded and validated the move towards fashion-led, off-the-peg clothes. It was the first ready-to-wear boutique to bear a couturier's name.

In 2001, Saint Laurent was appointed as a Commander of the Légion d'honneur.

Picasso-inspired knitwear, S/S 2012
Raf Simons for Jil Sander

Prints inspired by Vincent Van Gogh, S/S 2012
Rodarte

HOMAGE TO BRAQUE
YVES SAINT LAURENT
1988

Yves Saint Laurent (1936–2008) first forayed into art-inspired fashion with the Mondrian day dress that he designed in 1965, followed by his Pop art collection in 1966. For his haute couture collection in 1988, the designer featured tributes to the artists Henri Matisse, Vincent Van Gogh and Jean Cocteau. Simple in construction, the fitted single-breasted jackets—cropped to the waist and worn with narrow knee-length pencil skirts—acknowledged the structured shoulders and inverted triangle of the 1980s silhouette. Remarkable for their embellishment by the Parisian couture embroidery atelier Ecole Lesage, the garments are encrusted with layers of decorative stitching and beadwork of sequins and pearls, replicating the irises painted by Van Gogh and the patterning of Matisse. Referencing *The Two Birds*, painted by noted Cubist Georges Braque in 1956, two doves are embroidered on a back-fastening white gazar cape. Symbolic of love and peace—and therefore appropriate for a wedding gown—here, the circling doves are transformed by Saint Laurent into white cotton piqué, appliquéd to the bodice of the dress at the hip and breast, their beaks touchingly meeting at the waist. A smaller dove perches on the bride's head in place of a wedding veil. The traditional wedding train is represented by long white tulle streamers that flow from each wrist.

One of the most significant post-war designers, Saint Laurent trained at the school of the Chambre Syndicale de la Haute Couture before becoming assistant to Christian Dior and taking over the label after Dior's death in 1957. The Yves Saint Laurent label was founded with the designer's partner, Pierre Bergé, in 1962.

Designers look to the fine arts for inspiration, particularly the visual medium of painting, and images can be translated directly on to the surface of a garment, often by digital printing. Alternatively, more subtle homage is paid to the artist by means of colour and texture deployed by designers such as Mary Katrantzou and her embellished fabrics inspired by John Chamberlain's crushed-car sculptures.

Together with British designer Antony Price and fellow French designer Claude Montana, Mugler offered a slick, overtly glamorous sexuality through a heady combination of references, from sci-fi and futurism to the film noir of mid-century Hollywood. The 1980s was a period of high-gloss glamour and towering Amazonians, and the trio made formal dressing and immaculate grooming an imperative for a younger demographic, seen in the designers' identification with the music bands of the era and their cocktail vamp girlfriends.

Leather dress for the Roxy Music album cover For Your Pleasure, 1973
Antony Price

Peplum jacket, 1981
Claude Montana

AUTOMOTIVE CORSET DRESS
THIERRY MUGLER
1989

Exuding high-octane glamour mediated through 1950s Detroit car styling, the automotive corset dress by Thierry Mugler (1948–) reflects the designer's preoccupation with promulgating an Amazonian statement. Although the model lies back in an attitude of submission across the bonnet of a wrecked car, the dress is all streamlined angles and sharp edges, implying untouchability. The midriff features an automobile grille-shaped section, pointing downwards towards the crotch and upwards to the separation between the breasts. These are costumed as headlights: the red reflective surface is restricted to the centre of the breasts, while the upper and lower parts are held together with vertical metal hoops, resonant of outsize nipple clamps. The chrome-coloured outer edges of the edifice sweep upwards and outwards, like the extreme tail fins of a car, an accepted mark of luxury in 1950s motor-car design. The fins are also expressive of aerodynamic qualities, the implication being 'this woman can really move'. Further fins follow the angle at each side; they are tipped with red, like a stash of lipsticks, and a symbol of the dominatrix. In contrast, the simple narrow skirt is a silver sliver of light-reflecting sequins.

Mugler's approach to glamour—slashed hems, plunging necklines, spray-on tight skirts—reflects a parody of femininity with its emphasis on the secondary sexual characteristics, breasts, legs and hair.

During the 1980s, fetish fashion entered the mainstream. Mugler sculpted the toned female body into a fetishized superwoman, exaggerating her curves by deploying all the trappings of sadomasochism: leather corsets decorated with spikes and nipple rings, neck braces, rubber armour and towering heels. Boned and interfaced silk and satin evening gowns rendered the aesthetic less extreme.

The suit remains the most convincing of male garments. Whatever its diversity of detail or fabric, the suit's components remain constant: a jacket, a pair of trousers and occasionally a waistcoat, all cut from the same cloth. Suit design continues to evolve: trousers narrow or broaden, shoulders lose or gain padding, lapels widen or narrow, and jackets are vented or draped. Even when it is constructed from an ephemeral material such as paper, the man's business suit is an emblem of official power, suggesting a life free from physical toil and excess leisure.

This is a new take and look for a suit that, for us, represents the perfect link between art and fashion.

MARTY STAFF, PRESIDENT, HUGO BOSS

PAPER SUIT

JAMES ROSENQUIST FOR HUGO BOSS

1998

Produced with DuPont™ Tyvek®, a nonwoven fabric made from spunbonded olefin, the paper suit was designed by US pioneer of Pop art James Rosenquist (1933–) for menswear label Hugo Boss. The creation of the paper suit represented a continuation of the company's long-term collaboration with the Guggenheim Foundation, and it was introduced in March 1998 at the Deutsche Guggenheim in Berlin in conjunction with the exhibition of James Rosenquist's latest work, *The Swimmer in the Econo-Mist* (1997–98). Rosenquist was a contemporary of artists Claes Oldenburg, Roy Lichtenstein, Jasper Johns and Robert Rauschenberg, and his paper suit originated in 1966 with his desire for a throwaway tuxedo in order to avoid having to repeatedly rent one for his hectic social life. The 1960s also saw a brief flirtation with paper dresses, which were used to display the flat graphics of the era and were the perfect embodiment of the Pop art movement. With a limited edition of one hundred in brown and twenty-five in black, the suit is cut along conventional lines with a two-button jacket and narrow revers. The trousers are straight-cut and without turn-ups. Rosenquist signed and numbered a small, limited quantity of suits to be made available only through charity auctions.

The label achieved high visibility in the 1980s when the Hugo Boss suit epitomized the sartorial aspirations of the young ambitious professionals of the era. The brand has continued to expand into womenswear and sportswear. The strategy of subcontracting and the use of high-quality materials have enabled the brand to maintain visibility in a competitive market.

Hugo Boss AG is a high-profile fashion empire founded on the production of men's suits. It was established by Hugo Boss in 1924 in Metzingen, Germany, manufacturing workwear and uniforms up to and including World War II. The business expanded into menswear in 1953, its success predicated on the desire for middle-market, ready-to-wear suits with a fashionable edge. In 1993, the company was reorganized into a number of offshoots of the label, each with a cohesive, recognizable brand identity.

Paper dress with images of Hubert Humphrey, 1968
James Sterling

Concertina paper dress, 2010
Mauricio Velasquez Posada

Paper suit for men, 2010
Greg Lauren

The brand engaged in an early example of product placement when it appeared in the two most stylishly influential television shows of the 1980s: *Miami Vice* (1984–90) and *L.A. Law* (1986–94).

McQueen spearheaded an iconoclastic moment in fashion in the mid 1990s with his 'Dante' collection. After four years as chief designer at heritage house Givenchy, McQueen sold the majority shareholding of his own label to the Gucci Group in 2000, which provided a solid infrastructure for the designer.

**SPRAY-PAINT DRESS
ALEXANDER McQUEEN
1999**

Alexander McQueen (1969–2010) created fashion legend with a configuration of craft and technology for the finale of his untitled spring/summer show of 1999, in which former ballerina Shalom Harlow rotated on a mechanical plate, posing between two industrial robots from an Italian car factory. They performed a macabre dance, besmirching her virginal white gown with black and yellow sprayed paint. Inspired by an installation created by German artist Rebecca Horn, comprising two shotguns firing blood-red paint at each other, the staging was carefully choreographed for maximum impact. By the end of the showstopping performance, the dress and the model were splattered and dripping with paint in a spectacle that paid homage to Abstract Expressionist artist Jackson Pollock. The ballerina-length simple trapezoid line of the dress features many layers of silk tulle petticoats, gathered into a utilitarian broad leather saddlery strap held tight beneath the arms and fastened at the centre front with a square metal buckle. Another strap runs from side seam to side seam at the back, holding the dress close to the body. In contrast to the automatons, an undercurrent of craft precedes the spray-painted dress as the models revolve on the turntable clad in skirts made of perforated and segmented balsa wood and loose-weave raffia.

Relishing the spectacle of the runway show, McQueen perceived the arena as an opportunity to create avant-garde performance art. Eagerly anticipated, the dramatic scenarios evoked strong emotions: delight, disgust and awe.

Underlying the themes of implied savagery and glamour that frequently occurred throughout McQueen's provocative collections was a convincing display of technical virtuosity that underpinned the inherent drama with a commercial eye. The fashion show as performance art is common to designers such as Viktor & Rolf, whose 'Long Live the Immaterial' collection of 2002 used blue-screen technology, and to Comme des Garçons and Hussein Chalayan, who both favour a conceptual approach to fashion. The argument as to whether fashion is an art, a craft or a business is a continuing one.

Freehand painted tulle dress, 2008
Dolce & Gabbana

Jackson Pollock printed dress, S/S 2013
Duro Olowu

Ironic references to art, consumerism and politics are the remit of avant-garde designers such as Chalayan, Martin Margiela and Viktor & Rolf. All combine a point of view that renders the catwalk show not only another spectacle of seasonal trends, but also a thought-provoking intellectual exercise that challenges the viewer and is poised between performance and installation. The shows are frequently staged outside the usual arenas, occurring in venues such as derelict urban spaces, underground car parks and disused railway stations.

Secret dress collection, S/S 1999
Yohji Yamamoto

Marionette presentation, A/W 1999/2000
Maison Martin Margiela

SUGAR-GLASS DRESS
HUSSEIN CHALAYAN
2001

For his 'Ventriloquy' collection, visionary designer Hussein Chalayan (1970–) showed a short film in which the garments worn by computer-animated models mysteriously shattered. Live models then displayed a series of precisely tailored single-breasted jackets, worn over white shirts and knee-length skirts. Various pattern pieces on the jackets are marked in a different colour, presenting a more fluid version of the designer's aeroplane dress of 1999, in which sections of the garment come together to make the whole. Shades of denim are also patchworked into infinitely wearable cropped trousers and jackets. Bright orange pleated skirts and printed shifts inject colour to a neutral palette of tobacco brown, grey and khaki. Asymmetrical drawstring necklines feature on simple shift dresses and tops, partnered with knee-length skirts with a pronounced flounce. Betraying Chalayan's deconstruction ethos, flared and bell-shaped skirts in transparent silk organza show the marks of pattern-making. At the end of the show, in affirmation of the nature of commodity fetishism, the finale evokes the ephemerality of the fashion system: six models stand in pairs and one from each pair holds a mallet, which is used to break up the sugar-glass dresses.

Turkish-born Chalayan fronted knitwear company TSE from 1998 to 2001, and was creative director at British jeweler Asprey from 2001 to 2004. He became the Design Star Honoree in 2007.

Underpinning the artistic and cultural resonances of Chalayan's work, and his multilayered questions on the relationship of humanity to materiality, is a profound engagement with the craft of fashion and a commercially aware eye. This has sustained the designer throughout his career and has also resulted in more than fourteen international exhibitions of his work, including at the Venice Biennale in 2005.

Street clothing that meets the practical needs of an urban generation, providing physical protection in street protests and anonymity from CCTV surveillance, is a frequent source of inspiration for designers. Items include the hooded parka, garments with strategic padding over vulnerable areas and the use of high-performance fabrics that may include conductive fibres for sound and interactivity with the environment.

PROTECTIVE CLOTHING
BOUDICCA
2004

Nonconformist design duo Boudicca utilized the theme of the hunter-gatherer to cast a post-apocalyptic gloom over a collection of militaristic tailoring, transparent metallic nylon mackintoshes and sporty hooded jackets and track pants. In acknowledgement of the ancient British Iceni tribe, which was ruled by Queen Boudicca during the 1st century AD, the mostly utilitarian pieces in a sombre palette were enlivened by the use of fur collars and stoles thrown over the sharply cut monochrome coats. All the garments were shown against a desolate moorland backdrop, to the score of the cult movie *Badlands* (1973), directed by Terrence Malick. An overriding aspect of the show was the inclusion of protective clothing, including the loosely fitting white trousers and jacket resonant of World War I 'gasbags', a garment that tied at the waist, wrist and ankle to create a barrier impervious to toxic gas fumes. The jacket has a drawstring at the neck and the white fabric is interrupted with black flashes on each shoulder that match the black pockets on each side of centre front. A white wimple is left to hang either side of the face, in preparation for winding around the nose and mouth. A generous black turtle-neck sweater with over-the-hand sleeves is worn beneath the suit, as are knee-high black leather boots.

Following a fiercely uncompromising route, and with a commitment to continue the contextualization of fashion with art, the Boudicca label is fuelled by ideas rather than by commercial success. Although Boudicca articulates social comment through the medium of dress—with the designers investigating a dystopian world of untimely death, threatening technology and universal chaos—the label also continues to create life-affirming, cleverly considered concepts of cut and tailoring.

Vexed parka, 1995
Vexed Generation

Sequin safety vest,
A/W 2013/14
Ashish

Named after the queen of ancient Britain who led a revolt against the Roman army two thousand years ago, fashion label Boudicca was launched by Zowie Broach (1966–) and Brian Kirkby (1974–) in 1997. Boudicca was the first independent British fashion house to be invited to become a guest member of the Chambre Syndicale de la Haute Couture.

When Boudicca was formed in 1997, we envisioned it more as an art project than a fashion line.
BRIAN KIRKBY

Intensive research is integral to the Galliano aesthetic, and funds are allocated for the designer and a team of assistants to explore far-flung countries and other cultures. Ephemera such as street signs, market stalls and bus tickets have as much importance as museum treasures. Primary research is the most vital element of the creative process; it animates, inspires and directs all aspects of design development, in which decisions are made as to yarn, fabric, texture, palette, surface detail, decoration and silhouette.

'Planet Gaia' collection, 2010
Vivienne Westwood

'Mexican Outworkers' collection, 2010
Rodarte

NEWSPRINT
JOHN GALLIANO
2004

Providing a density of visual messages inspired by the seafarers of the Yemeni tribes of western Asia, John Galliano (1960–) combines an extravagantly wide crinoline with the accoutrements of a tribe on the move. A felt hat is perched on top of a floral headscarf tied at the back, Romani style, with a canteen of miniature pots and pans hanging amid lustrous locks of fake hair. The designer's signature newsprint, a specially written newspaper printed on cloth by fellow Central Saint Martins College of Arts and Design graduates Stephanie Nash and Anthony Michael, is fashioned into a 3.5 metre-wide (12 ft) skirt of overlapping layers. The close-fitting jacket is cut along the lines of a spencer, a style that dates from the 1790s and was later adopted as a mess jacket by British military officers, thus referencing the period when the Yemen came under British rule in the 19th century. The jacket is single-breasted, fastened with a row of brass buttons and cropped at the waist. Red piping delineates the high-standing collar and the flaps of the breast pockets, sited above two double parallel seams shaped to the waist. Taking the footloose, grab-as-you-go scavenger look to its extreme, the feet are encased in plastic carrier bags.

But I'm not an artist. Maybe an artist with a small 'a'.

Galliano secured a cult following with collections such as 'Afghanistan Repudiates Western Ideals' (1985), which brought him international recognition and led to an invitation by Bernard Arnault of LVMH to head the Parisian house Givenchy in 1995, the first British designer invited to head a couture house. Galliano reached the apotheosis of his success at the house of Dior, from which he was summarily dismissed in 2011.

? Although the seemingly chaotic mixes seen in Galliano's runway shows might be perceived as outrageous or impracticable, amid the postmodern pastiche and romantic fantasies are garments grounded in the designer's innovative tailoring and cutting expertise. Alongside the haute bohemia for Dior, Galliano's collections for his own label consolidate his creative identity, while also reaching a different demographic.

Pugh's inherently theatrical approach to design has its provenance in his background in costume design: he worked for the English National Youth Theatre from the age of fourteen. Combined with the extremes of club culture—there are echoes of performance artist Leigh Bowery in his approach— Pugh's fabricated silhouettes, inevitably confined to a palette of grey, black and white, place him at the forefront of designers who combine performance art and fashion.

Black-and-white gimp suit,
1990s
Leigh Bowery

Houndstooth check dress,
A/W 2013/14
McQ by Alexander McQueen

CHECK WRAP COAT
GARETH PUGH
2007

Gareth Pugh (1981–) incorporates his familiar codes of gimp masks, inflated PVC and aggressive silhouettes in a collection purportedly inspired by Ridley Scott's fantasy movie *Legend* (1985). The chequerboard pattern features throughout, with variations in size and texture of the black-and-white check. Here, outsize chequerboard squares are worked into a wrap coat, the model's head set between monstrously huge and threatening shoulders that extend out to twice the width of the body. Cropped at the knee, with wide sleeves ending above the wrist, the coat is worn over an all-enveloping black rubber catsuit. The chequerboard pattern is also used for a cashmere dress in which the squares increase in size towards the hem, adding emphasis to the undulating folds of the skirt. Its 1950s glamour is perversely subverted by the model's black rubber mask with barely there air holes and eyeholes. Tight-fitting gimp masks, some of them sprouting ponytails or strange rubber excrescences, render all the models genderless and featureless. These accompany a series of fantastic architectonic constructions fashioned from patchworked squares of black-and-white vinyl, square plastic paillettes used to create overlapping scales and silver-and-black checked foil.

> *If I were to do the big shapes I do, colour would maybe be too much. Pink or red would push it all over the edge.*

The British-born designer's first solo show appeared at London Fashion Week in 2006, sponsored by NEWGEN, and the following year his collections went on sale for the first time. In 2008, he presented his first show in Paris, followed by his first menswear show in Paris in 2009. Pugh's first stand-alone store opened in Hong Kong in August 2010.

? The juxtaposition of black and white in pattern is always graphically compelling, as seen in the classic houndstooth signature check of couture house Dior and the Op art dazzle of 1960s fashion. Striped, spotted or checked, black and white chime with our innate perceptions of the monochromatic transitions in our environment. We prioritize the reading of light and shade with the same primitive mechanisms as protozoa.

At Balenciaga, Ghesquière combined couture-level handwork with a pragmatic appreciation of the market, thus sustaining the prominence of the house while giving it a modern edge. Here, he uses a pre-fall collection to elaborate on ideas before committing them to the more commercially significant seasonal collections. This mix of experimentation and luxury, which included a template of sculptural simplicity and an element of rock 'n' roll, translates into a personal aesthetic that he now brings to Louis Vuitton as creative director.

Fur muff and cuffs, 1950s
Chanel

Fuchsia-dyed fur coat,
A/W 2000/01
Versace

SLIP DRESS AND FUR MITTENS
BALENCIAGA
2009

Incorporating all the codes of a creative director, Nicolas Ghesquière (1971–) includes draping, cocoon-shaped dropped-shoulder jackets, high-waisted peplums and the influential jodhpur trouser: skinny pants with a high-waisted top, pleated into width on the hips, and a slightly dropped crotch. Among the sportswear-inspired parkas in high-tech fabrics, the designer offers evening wear in neutral-coloured silks and satins that have a chemise-like feel. Here, Ghesquière introduces a minimal slip of a dress that is resonant of Mariano Fortuny, the early 20th-century master of the pleated neoclassical dress. The bodice in lustrous silver panne velvet is simply cut with a bound open 'V'-shape neckline and set-in sleeves. The matt soft gathers of the skirt, divided from the top with a band of apricot silk ribbon, fall from a high waist with volume at the hem. Over-the-elbow black fur mittens add an unexpected note. The top-handle handbag in greige, with minimal metal hardware, is an important commercial adjunct to the collection, as are the distinctive boots. The heavy tread of the sole, the high gloss of the leather and the chunky buckled strap are in sharp contrast to the ethereal dress, which is accessorized with a drop crystal, loosely slung around the neck.

I want to please myself first. I'm always very stressed about making a new proposition every season.
NICOLAS GHESQUIÈRE

Ghesquière was an intern at Agnès B while still at school, and also interned with avant-garde designer Jean Paul Gaultier. He joined Balenciaga in 1995 as a licensed product designer, and in 1997 he was appointed as the label's new creative director. During his fifteen-year tenure, he successfully repositioned the house as one of the most influential brands.

The disturbing and erotic power of fur when it is used for any reason other than protection and warmth is seen as a surreal transposition that evokes an element of shock, if not horror. It also provokes sexual arousal in the fur obsessive. When fur is juxtaposed with over-the-elbow mittens, the fetishist is further excited, gloves being a recognized fetish item and an object of inappropriate yearning.

?

Resolutely outside mainstream design and flouting all recognizable fashion codes, Margiela subverted the rational approach to garment construction by pushing the boundaries between performance, art installation and fashion. His determination to create new meanings in fashion characterized him as an iconoclast who nevertheless remained a paradigm of intellectual integrity and of continuing relevance.

HAIR COAT
MAISON MARTIN MARGIELA
2009

Worm-filled corset, S/S 1996
Alexander McQueen

Faux blood-streaked dress,
A/W 2008/09
Rodarte

The impossibility of defining the boundaries between the hair of the model and the hair of the coat gives rise to the disquieting question: which is the living material and which the dead? The fact that the hair on the head is a wig, and therefore also fake, only adds to the conundrum. Such puzzles are an intrinsic element of the aesthetic of Maison Martin Margiela, a Paris-based label launched by Belgian-born deconstructivist Martin Margiela (1957–) in 1989 and renowned for its conceptual rigour. The hair of the coat has a dual function, as a fetish object and as a garment component; it is not only attractive because of its surface lustre, but also grotesque and repulsive at the same time. Here, it is placed out of context by the designer, who upholds various tenets of the Surrealist art movement, which deals with displacement and the unfamiliar in a familiar setting. The wig is carefully coiffed into a deep fringe and 'flicks', and it is a slightly deeper shade of blonde than the coat. Equally unsettling is the model's face, blanked out by a dark brown stocking scarf that renders her anonymous, much like the secretive and publicity-shy Margiela. The body is nearly nude beneath the thigh-length edge-to-edge coat, garbed only in a brief pair of pants worn under sheer tights pulled up to a high waist.

Margiela studied at Antwerp's Royal Academy of Fine Arts alongside the experimental fashion collective the Antwerp Six, which included Dries Van Noten and Ann Demeulemeester. A freelance designer for five years from 1980, Margiela worked for Jean Paul Gaultier between 1985 and 1987 before launching his own label.

In contrast to his avant-garde approach to design, Margiela was hired in 1997 by Jean-Louis Dumas to supervise women's ready-to-wear at the traditional luxury house Hermès, where he remained until 2003.

The hair coat appeared in Margiela's twentieth anniversary collection, a reminder of the designer's challenging contribution to fashion. His experimental practice featured the deconstruction not only of couture techniques but also of the fashion system itself. Earlier work included two semi-couture collections based on the tailor's dummy, describing stages of the production process with sections of the toile permanently attached to the piece.

De Castelbajac is known as JC/DC by his hip-hop fans but he is also a French nobleman. He has a hyperactive approach to appropriating the colourful and the comic to produce accessible, fun-filled clothing. This provides red-carpet appeal to a younger demographic, and his designs are favoured by Lady Gaga and Katy Perry, the latter of whom wore a royal-blue satin sheath with Betty Boop eyes for bra cups to the MTV Awards in 2008.

My biggest inspiration is the strength of image. These images can come from popular culture or high art.

Couture collection, S/S 1966
Yves Saint Laurent

Warhol-print evening dress, 1991
Versace

WARHOL DRESS
JEAN-CHARLES DE CASTELBAJAC
2009

Returning to his familiar trope of Pop art and one of his major influences, Andy Warhol, Jean-Charles de Castelbajac (1949–) imprints a sequinned larger-than-life image of the artist's well-known face on to the front of a minidress, complete with a Warhol-like, bleached-out, candyfloss wig. This forms the deep collar of the dress, falling almost to the waist and covering the shoulders. A tuft of black natural hair sprouting below the wig adds authenticity, and is an effect that is replicated on all the runway models. In a collection that includes images of Clint Eastwood in a fright wig and Michael Jackson with an Afro, the designer also hijacks, with his customary wit and tongue-in-cheek approach, a number of Jim Henson's Muppets for the runway, including Kermit the Frog declaiming Shakespeare. The cadaverous features of Warhol are described in Ben-Day dots, a printing process dating from 1879 and named after illustrator and printer Benjamin Henry Day Jr. The technique was favoured by US Pop art practitioner Roy Lichtenstein, who enlarged and exaggerated the dots in many of his paintings and sculptures. The monochrome heavily made-up face of the artist is silhouetted on black, and the 1960s-inspired minidress is worn over black opaque tights for a full-on beat effect.

The De Castelbajac label went into receivership in 2011 after its owner, the Sixth Swedish National Pension Fund, decided to withdraw its investment. The same year, the South Korean firm EXR bought the company outright and appointed De Castelbajac as artistic director. It launched a third line, 'Ligne', which the designer describes as 'French preppy'.

The prolific output of Warhol, Pop art's best-known practitioner, and his significance as the superstar of the New York arts and social scene in the 1960s have resulted in familiarity with the artist's haunted gaze and wild hair. Replicating Warhol's own silk-screen reproductions of US icons such as Jacqueline Kennedy and Marilyn Monroe, images of the artist continue to abound in contemporary fashion as shorthand for a pop sensibility and in acknowledgement of his wide-reaching influence.

? Wit and humour are rarely allied to avant-garde fashion. This generally has serious intentions and is produced alongside an intellectually rigorous manifesto. Fashion that is merely playful is nevertheless valid, offering a light-hearted view of the possibilities inherent in the construction and presentation of a garment. Its noteworthiness often underpins a brand's excursion into fragrance and accessories.

UMBRELLA SUIT
AGATHA RUÍZ DE LA PRADA
2009

In a witty inversion of the umbrella, so that it catches the rain rather than provides protection, idiosyncratic designer Agatha Ruíz de la Prada y Sentmenat (1960–) enlivens the catwalk with her surreal jokes. These include giant fried eggs on a gingham tablecloth dress, accessorized with a baguette balanced precariously on the model's head, and a fuchsia-pink puffball dress to which an oversized purple moustache has been appliquéd, in honour of her inspiration, artist Salvador Dalí. Polychromatic outfits feature brick-wall-print all-in-ones, covered with appliquéd fake flowers and an inset birdcage, complete with bird. The tailoring of the jacket of the umbrella suit is conventional; it is single-breasted with a slanted breast pocket and a single-button fastening in the shape of a heart, a signature motif of the brand. It is paired with a traditional shirt and tie. Cut from a hot-pink silk velvet, the upturned umbrella starts at mid thigh and reaches up towards the waist, each prong ending with a round red glass bead. Shiny plastic tear-shaped balloons in blue are suspended artfully from the umbrella, in a facsimile of a shower of raindrops. The legs are encased in an opaque pearlized pale purple, giving the appearance of plastic.

A charismatic figure in Madrid's cultural life, Ruíz de la Prada promoted the *Movida Madrileña*, an artistic movement that emerged in the 1970s, and in 1993 she organized a salon, where intellectuals and artists met at her studio. These activities inform her aesthetic, which combines humour with a surrealistic displacement of objects, an approach that extends to her various art, fashion and interior projects. The designer's often outlandish and rainbow-hued catwalk shows are some of the most anticipated in Europe.

Sky dress, 2010
3lectromode

Black umbrella dress, A/W 2011/12
Knapp

The Spanish-born designer presented her first womenswear collection in 1981 in Madrid, and subsequently showed in France, Italy, South America, New York and Japan. In 1991, the label expanded into menswear and childrenswear, ceramics, toys, shoes, linens, towels and cosmetics, retailed through the brand's exclusive stores in Madrid, Barcelona, Paris, Milan, New York, Oporto and Majorca.

Colour is the common bond between all of my creations. . .if you put colour in your life, you become happier, saner, more joyful.

Creating a bridge between Eastern and Western art and earning global recognition with an Oscar, a Grammy and a number of other honours, Manhattan-based Ishioka brought a dramatic gothic Surrealism with elements of the erotic to an extensive range of productions.

This included a series of groundbreaking, subversive, anti-product commercials, featuring Hollywood actress Faye Dunaway, for Parco (an upmarket Japanese department store), and the costume designs for Francis Ford Coppola's *Bram Stoker's Dracula*, for which she won an Academy Award in 1992.

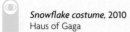

Snowflake costume, 2010
Haus of Gaga

Exotic bird costume, 2011
Cee Lo Green

BACKLESS DRESS
EIKO ISHIOKA
2009

On-stage drama was the inevitable result of a creative collaboration between renowned diva Grace Jones and avant-garde Japanese designer and art director Eiko Ishioka (1938–2012). For the singer's 'Hurricane Tour' in 2009, Ishioka designed a series of dramatic costumes that showcased Grace's powerfully gym-honed body and fearsome visage in a number of showstopping outfits. These included her manifestation as a warrior queen in a second-skin bodysuit printed with zebra stripes, topped with an outsize stylized plumed helmet that incorporated a white nylon knee-length wig. A wide, panniered skirt attached to a deeply plunging corset was worn with thigh-high gold boots and a gold face mask, and a silk-satin cape billowed out behind the singer to cover the entire stage. Here, for her performance of 'La Vie En Rose', the singer is costumed with all the fiery influence of flamenco in a very specific dark and intense shade of scarlet, reportedly a colour that Ishioka favoured above all others. The concentric circles are stiffened and dagged to give the impression of flames, an effect that is enhanced during the performance by being lit from beneath. As the diva rotates on a turntable, the dress is revealed to be completely backless; her body appears as if naked apart from a thong.

> *I don't know if it's beauty or not. . . . It is from my point of view, and I always want to create my own kind of beauty.*

A multifaceted designer, Ishioka graduated in 1961 from Tokyo University of the Arts, or Geidai, where she trained as a graphic designer before working for cosmetics company Shiseido. Considered Japan's foremost art director, she was responsible for the costume design for the opening ceremony of the 2008 Summer Olympic Games in Beijing.

Ishioka set the paradigm for extreme stage and film costumes, pushing the boundaries of the acceptable and the possible with the authenticity of a visionary intelligence. A persuasive image-maker, the designer influenced a generation of pop provocateurs, such as Lady Gaga and Madonna, and introduced the notion of a performance in which music, fashion and stage set form an integrated whole.

? The characters of the commedia dell'arte are a fruitful source of inspiration to designers. They include Harlequin, with his diamond-checked jacket and coat, seen in 1989 in Vivienne Westwood's 'Voyage to Cythera' knitwear collection; Pantalone, who gave his name to loosely fitting trousers that tie at the ankle; and Pulcinella, who wears a smock top decorated with a row of outsize pom-poms.

PIERROT COSTUME
AMAYA ARZUAGA
2009

Referencing the sad clown Pierrot from the commedia dell'arte, a theatrical form popularized in the late 17th century by Italian travelling troupes of players and the origin of contemporary circus, Madrid-based designer Amaya Arzuaga (1970–) repositions the deep frilled ruff of stiffened organza, more usually worn to frame the face, to just above the knees. Here, it creates a short, almost horizontal skirt, the obverse of the rigid and padded upturned frame above. This gives the impression of changing the proportions of the body, creating a disjointed, acrobatic figure by implying two indented waists—a shift in the silhouette that occurs throughout the collection. The undulating wired edges of the organza frill in pale silver grey are decorated with swathes of ruched black and purple silk-satin ribbon, interspersed with matching rosettes. The deep purple strapless bodice in light-reflecting sequins is moulded to the body before flaring out into yet another stiffened peplum-length skater skirt. The waist is emphasized by a broad black silk-satin cummerbund tied at the back in an outsize obi-like bow. Beneath the frilled and stiffened skirts is a pair of loose pantaloon-type trousers, in silk tulle and caught in at the ankle, by fellow Spanish designer Armand Basi. These are worn above high wedge-heeled shoes by Italian label Moschino.

Arzuaga joined her parent's fashion company, Elipse, before launching her own label in 1994; two years later she won the Spanish Designer of the Year Award. After initially showing her collections at various fashion fairs, Arzuaga made her runway debut at London Fashion Week in 1997.

Roundabout skirt, 2009
Manish Arora

Pierrot collared suit, S/S 2013
Walter Van Beirendonck

Haute couture Pierrot,
A/W 2011/12
Dior

In 2005, in recognition of her services to fashion, Arzuaga was distinguished with the Medalla de Oro al Mérito en las Bellas Artes by King Juan Carlos and the Cultural Ministry of Spain.

Applying geometry to her layered compositions through sculpted silk satin and artfully cut and draped silk chiffon, Arzuaga concentrates on occasion and evening wear in rich, jewel-like colours. The designer's aesthetic encompasses the avant-garde, with excursions into fibre optics and sculptural infrastructures that support unusual silhouettes. These appear alongside more commercial pieces, such as strapless evening gowns and short flirty cocktail dresses.

Until 2013, long-time co-worker, stylist and personal friend of Gaga, Nicola Formichetti was responsible for styling many of the performer's most outrageous stage costumes, but he has since been replaced by Brandon Maxwell. In addition to showcasing the talents of her creative team, Gaga also calls upon avant-garde designers such as Thierry Mugler and Hussein Chalayan, the latter of whom constructed the translucent womb from which the singer emerged at the 53rd Annual Grammy Awards held in 2011.

Rib-cage corset, S/S 1998
Shaun Leane for Alexander McQueen

Laser-cut ribbed bodice, S/S 2009
Rodarte

SKELETON SHOW COSTUME
HAUS OF GAGA
2009

The bone pleather dress is one of many seemingly absurd creations worn on stage by pop performance artist Lady Gaga in her continual attempt to shock, astound and confuse her audiences. Driven by the necessity for reinvention, Gaga visits a multiplicity of personas for her stage appearances. Flesh-coloured, high-waisted spandex pants and an all-encompassing bra top are the foundation for the ribbed armature of the pleather structure, which forms a brief bolero around the upper body. A flesh-pink 'T' strap circles the waist and is attached with rows of reinforced running stitch to two broad bands of what appears to be strips of old-fashioned, plaster-like stretch fabric. With all the seductive appeal of a misplaced bandage, these are in the same shade of flesh pink and anchored at the thigh, held in place with an inner strap of the same material, creating an uneasy confluence at the groin. The structure encases Gaga's pale translucent skin, interrupted only by the tight mesh of the fishnet stockings. Lustrous, putty-coloured patent boots, laced at the front and with a high spindly heel, are like a carapace beneath the bones of a strange beast, arching over the ankles and feet like a predatory, long-dead animal. In contrast, the maquillage and hair are blonde-bombshell style.

[Andy] Warhol. . .was able to make commercial art that was taken seriously as fine art. . .that's what I'm doing too.

LADY GAGA

Modelled after Andy Warhol's Factory studio in New York, which combined the plastic and moving arts under one roof, the Haus of Gaga is a collective of multidisciplinary practitioners of film, media, set and costume design. This personal creative team devises the concepts for the singer's live performances and other visual representations of her work.

Placing the skeleton outside the body and transforming it into a high-fashion object was first mooted by Elsa Schiaparelli with her Surrealist-inspired dress from 1938 (see pp. 58–59). British set designer and illustrator Gary Card reinvents this idea for the 21st century with the skeleton show costume for the 'Monster Ball Tour', in which Lady Gaga exploits this symbol of death and decay in a highly sexualized performance, which she claims was based on the theme of evolution.

Eary studied for her MA at London's Royal College of Art and graduated in 2008, immediately securing an entry in British *Vogue* with garments photographed by Mario Testino and worn by Kate Moss. The designer launched her menswear label in 2009 and her womenswear label in 2013, featuring second-skin garments in vibrant prints. Eary has also produced a collection of swimwear based on her knowledge of body contour fashion, which she studied at the University of Leicester.

Bodysuit showing circulatory system, A/W 1998/99
Olivier Theyskens

Knitted rib cage, S/S 2008
Gareth Pugh

BODY PARTS
KATIE EARY
2010

The fashion designer as an anatomist is a common occurrence on the catwalk: aspects of the body are increasingly used as a source of inspiration for collections, whether as a fearsome memento mori or as fuel to shock. Literally showing the inside outside, London-based menswear designer Katie Eary (1983–) prefers a more humorous approach and eschews the gruesome for a spring/summer collection titled 'Naked Lunch', inspired by William Burroughs's classic novel of the same name (1959). The body is represented in layers from the bones up: the skin-coloured all-in-one features the skeleton; the loose-fitting T-shirt is printed with anatomically correct images of body parts, including a heart and images of the circulatory system; and pearls, rhinestones and chains, with an emphasis on gold, form rib cages. The red distressed baggy Bermuda shorts are worn over the all-in-one and gold-coloured flat sandals take the form of skeletal feet, thereby matching the skeleton hand jewelry. Lengths of red mountaineering rope are coiled elaborately around the shoulders, representing wayward blood vessels, and joke goggles, designed in collaboration with luxury eyewear designer Linda Farrow, are perched below a metallic half mask shaped like a skull.

Following the success of the skeleton show, Eary was approached by US rapper Kanye West; she was employed to work on his collections as creative lead for two seasons.

One of the few female designers producing menswear, Eary was initially extreme, ebullient and idiosyncratic in her approach. Since her debut, the designer has extended her range to include the use of bold digital polychromatic placement and all-over prints combined with simple statement pieces such as Crombie coats with matching trousers.

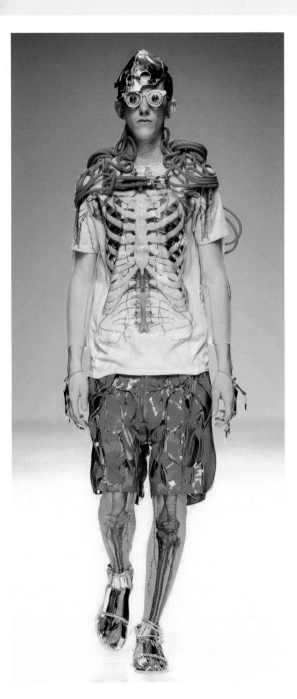

? Eary's use of anatomy as an art form, rather than for educational purposes, questions the boundaries between contemporary fashion and applied and fine art. By exposing muscle and body parts, albeit with a clear sense of irony, the designer is following in the tradition of artists such as Damien Hirst, who created the monumental work *Hymn* (1999–2005)—a polychrome bronze sculpture based on the Young Scientist Anatomy Set designed by Roman Emms—and Gunther von Hagens, the controversial German anatomist, who plastinated bodies and exhibited them worldwide.

"

I believe that men invented 'feminism' but disguised this word as dandy or fop.

? Mundane subject matter is appropriated frequently by fashion designers and it is either transmuted into abstract designs, so that it becomes virtually unrecognizable, or the object is arranged in such a manner that it loses its significance. In this way, the resulting pattern becomes more important than the object, and is further removed when constructed into a three-dimensional garment.

SURREAL PRINT DRESS GILES 2010

British-born designer Giles Deacon (1969–) transforms a mundane office staple, the paperclip, into an evening gown of sensual elegance that epitomizes the designer's idiosyncratic approach to fashion. The all-over print of interlocking, outsize paperclips in black and white creates a surface pattern in which the subject matter is almost unidentifiable. Further exploiting the motif, the broad black satin shoulder straps scroll around the breasts like a paperclip unwound. Intimations of the boudoir are apparent in the swansdown powder puff tucked into the waist-defining black ribbon, secured with a rhinestone buckle. The sensuous lines of the body-skimming silhouette and the luxurious fall of satin over the hips are resonant of the Hollywood screen sirens of the 1930s, an era that is also recalled by the incorporation of surreal imagery into elegant evening wear, popularized at the time by French couturière Elsa Schiaparelli. The paperclip motif recurs on the spectacular Stephen Jones construction that adorns the model's head. Deacon emphasizes the juxtaposition of rough and smooth by presenting fifteen pieces of his pre-fall collection in the factory where the renowned Richard Ginori porcelain is produced, surrounding the garments with piles of bowls and plates against a rough-hewn backdrop of wooden pallets and iron girders.

Tears dress, 1938
Schiaparelli

Lip print dress, 2011
Prada

Tin-can print, S/S 2011
Mary Katrantzou

The Deacon collection is always a little bit sideways. British in feel. . .quirky. I don't design for wallflowers.
GILES DEACON

Deacon has fine-tuned his democratic approach to fashion, designing for high-end labels and collaborating with high-street retailers. Combining high art and popular culture, he juxtaposes realism with fantasy, habitually incorporating whimsical references to cartoon figures, such as Pac-Man, in his collections. Bold prints featuring unusual ephemera and a playful disregard for the rules are matched to a singular respect for bespoke textiles and materials.

After graduating, Deacon worked with Jean-Charles de Castelbajac in Paris for two years. From 1998 to 2002, he was creative head of luxury goods label Bottega Veneta, and in 2004 presented his first collection at London Fashion Week. He was creative director at couture house Ungaro from 2010 to 2011.

? The shift from mechanical screen-printing to the computer manipulations of digital printing has extended the designer's potential to create complex combinations of colour and pattern. Katrantzou's innovative use of this process is in part responsible for its reappraisal as a legitimate means of expression. Thanks to the influence of Katrantzou and the adoption of the latest technological advances in computer-led design, the digital printing process is now considered a new medium in its own right, rather than a poor relation to the hands-on craft of screen-printing.

"

I'm inspired by women who have that travelled, refined eye. . .women who can blur the line between design and art.

TYPEWRITER DRESS
MARY KATRANTZOU
2012

Print maximalist Mary Katrantzou (1983–) integrates a complicated two-dimensional pattern into a marvel of three-dimensional trompe l'oeil, rendering a 1960s-style typewriter in Olivetti red into a piece of wearable sculpture. An eclectic confluence of references includes aspects of Elizabethan dress from the 16th century, evident in the structured silhouette and the square-cut corseted bodice. A Qwerty keyboard is incorporated into the yoke, complete with space bar and shift keys, and is framed by the moulded carriage-return levers. In a pastiche of the Elizabethan partlet (a neck and shoulder covering), an image of the type bars is used to give the impression of a pleated or goffered frill from the edge of the bodice to the neckline. The stiffened peplum is lined with an embellished keyboard print, which divides at the dipped waist before curving back in on itself to create a silhouette resonant of the flat-topped crinoline. The Rococo swirls of the printed velvet intensify on the lower bodice of the dress and become more diffuse on the stiff folds of the mid-thigh skirt. The edge of the heavily textured godet inserted into the centre front of the skirt is decorated in faux typewriter ribbon, embellished with rhinestone keys. The sharply tailored shoulder line adds to the rigidity of the silhouette.

One of a group of designers exploiting the potential of digital printing, Katrantzou engineers intricate hyperreal images and enriches the surface with her signature beaded and embroidered embellishment. Her maximalist aesthetic combines an eclectic range of references with a silhouette that is constantly refreshed from overly structured to free-floating.

Born in Athens, Katrantzou left Greece to study architecture at Rhode Island School of Design before moving to London. The designer first explored trompe l'oeil with her postgraduate collection, and launched her eponymous label in 2008 to universal acclaim. Katrantzou has a strong commercial eye and has built up a collection of simplified pieces, including knitwear, to support the statement wear luxe end of the label, which is bought by collectors or purchased as museum pieces.

Caravan digital print,
A/W 2010/11
Basso & Brooke

Embellished jacket, 2012
Proenza Schouler

Waterfall dress, 2013
Peter Pilotto

The Parisian couture embroidery house Ecole Lesage collaborated with Katrantzou for autumn/winter 2012/13; it was the first time the atelier had worked with a London designer.

Quick to refute allegations of androgyny, Anderson is unequivocal that his menswear is authentically unisex; the intention is a shared wardrobe rather than a transgressive statement about cross-dressing.

The designer repositions menswear in a way that is unprecedented in fashion history, with a new line that is equally effective when worn by women. Pieces that debuted on the men's runway were reintroduced in the women's collection, virtually unchanged but for a few fitting details, and worn by models of similar stature.

Hipster skater skirts for men and women, 1960s
Rudi Gernreich

Draped skirt, S/S 2012
Rick Owens

In 2013, luxury goods conglomerate LVMH acquired a minority stake in the J. W. Anderson label. The designer was appointed creative director of Spanish leather house Loewe as part of the deal.

**FRILLED SHORTS
J. W. ANDERSON
2013**

When British designer J. W. Anderson (1984–) introduced frilled shorts into his fourth menswear collection alongside kangaroo-pocket tube tops and thigh-length minidresses, he created a furore in the press.

Channelling the pared-down, minimal aesthetic of the 1960s, in this example the designer creates a flattened two-dimensional silhouette, which crosses the gender divide by introducing feminine details to a top and shorts combo. The bifurcation of the shorts is covert, hidden by the rigid circular frills at the hem. These give the appearance of a skater skirt, emphasized by the brevity of the shorts and the fluted silhouette. In addition, the shorts appear groinless: the fly front is unobtrusive and there are none of the details usually seen in the traditional men's trouser, such as pleats from a waistband. The fabric is rigid, unyielding and bonded to sponge for volume, resulting in the square-shaped top standing away from the body, an effect that is also seen in the tailored sleeves. Minute tucks in the neckline create a carapace-like front to the slip-over top, highlighted by the use of resistant fabric. Styled up with matching frills on the knee-length boots and slicked-back hair, the look is uncompromising and assertive.

Born in Northern Ireland, Jonathan William Anderson launched his menswear brand in 2008 after studying at the London College of Fashion; his womenswear line followed two years later. The designer has overseen two successful Topshop collections, and a one-off capsule collection for Versus, Versace's second line. Anderson won the Emerging Talent Award in 2012 at the British Fashion Awards.

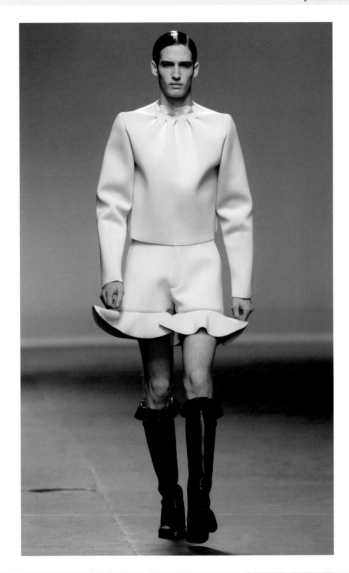

Previously skirts for men had been one of two styles: the almost macho wrapped and pleated kilt variety—worn with hefty boots and a six pack—or the sculptural drapes and folds of the Japanese designers. Anderson's frilled shorts feature in a collection that represents a new line of minimal crisp tailoring in neutral colours—grey, white and black—with the odd shot of cobalt, uninterrupted by print or pattern.

The appropriation of animal skins has a long, complex association with fashion. Abstract interpretations of their patterning and the use of the skins themselves have existed since the origins of clothing. Rarer is the use of pictorial, realistic imagery. Particularly prevalent are portrayals of the big cats, such as leopard and cheetah, popularized in the 1980s by Japanese label Kenzo. More recently, British designer Bella Freud has initiated a trend for dogs rendered in intarsia knitwear.

OUTSIZE FOX-HEAD DRESS
JEAN-CHARLES DE CASTELBAJAC
2013

With a collection titled 'Foxy Lady', the designer inevitably has to include a literal version of the vulpine beast, particularly if the collection belongs to Moroccan-born Jean-Charles de Castelbajac (1949–), for four decades a fashion maverick. Not for him the nuance or the subtle reference, but an Alice in Wonderland world of surreal juxtaposition. The blanket-check dress, to which De Castelbajac has returned continually in his collections since he cut his first jacket from a boarding-school blanket at the age of seventeen, is woven in a coarse outsize jacquard that is more usually used for figurative textiles. A larger-than-life fox's head in shades of grey, black and white, and with a benign and unchallenging expression, is featured prominently at the front of the dress. The fox's head is lightly padded to create a three-dimensional effect, and it forms a triangular bodice that reaches from the lower waist of the model up to the neckline, thus creating a sleeve for the upper arms. The design subsequently continues outwards, extending beyond the shoulder line, and the tips of the fox's ears are level with the model's ears. The detailed image of the face is achieved through the weaving of long floats in the weft, and aided by finer yarns in the warp to give the appearance of an embroidered satin-stitch. The thigh-high minidress in monochrome tweed is banded at the hem with a deep ruched border.

With a career in fashion that spans more than thirty years De Castelbajac remains a pioneer of the avant-garde. His vibrant and colourful approach has accrued various commissions, which include dressing Madonna and being the surprise choice for the role of official designer for the World Youth Day celebrations, held in Paris in 1997. De Castelbajac created the papal vestments and dressed 5,000 priests in rainbow-motif robes.

When I was a kid I was living my adolescence, and when adolescent I was like an adult. So I believe my time for childhood is now.

De Castelbajac launched his label in Paris in 1975 and achieved immediate recognition as one of the foremost designers of the new prêt-à-porter. He became a member of the Chambre Syndicale de la Haute Couture in 1978.

Animal motif sweaters, 1980s
Krizia

'Horse' collection, S/S 2001
Stella McCartney for Chloé

Leopard head fur,
A/W 2012/13
Karl Lagerfeld for Fendi

A former actor, Browne worked at Giorgio Armani's showroom in New York in 1998 and as a merchandiser at Club Monaco. He opened a bespoke tailoring shop in Manhattan's Tribeca neighbourhood in 2001 and introduced a men's ready-to-wear collection in 2004. Collaborations include the 'Black Fleece' line with Brooks Brothers. Browne received the Council of Fashion Designers of America Menswear Designer of the Year Award in 2006 and 2013, and was named the GQ Designer of the Year in 2008.

Brocade coat, A/W 2013/14
Etro

Madras-check short suit,
S/S 2014
Comme des Garçons

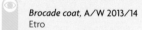

MULTIPATTERNED COAT

THOM BROWNE

2013

Thom Browne (1965–) wholeheartedly disrupts the stereotypes of conventional menswear and indulges in a game of fashion fantasy with bold colours and frantically patterned fabrics. Widely recognized by a series of awards for acts of bravado in the cut, proportions and materials of his sharp tailoring since his label debut in 2001, Browne continues to take liberties with the trappings of normality in this spring/summer collection. The designer toys wildly with menswear expectations by pitting boldly imaged fabric against boldly imaged fabric and by inflicting amputation on sleeve and trouser lengths. The formal collar and revers of a Crombie-style short coat are traduced by a naive polychromatic print of 1960s Pop art vivacity, featuring stylized whales, which is almost matched to the pattern of the tailored Bermuda shorts. The undersleeve of the coat has a fully constructed tailored cuff, and its two-colour print is more sparse. Layered beneath the coat is a pale aqua cardigan, fastened with a single feature button, and a madras-check shirt competes with a technicolour regimental stripe tie. The schoolboy prankster that is Browne cannot resist the temptation to play like an extraterrestrial tourist in the transgender wardrobe and with fabrics of the modern era.

In 2008, Browne was appointed by French skiwear company Moncler to design 'Gamme Bleu', the men's counterpart to its women's couture line, 'Gamme Rouge'.

With slim-cut suits and cropped trousers, Browne initially offered a subversive version of the late 1950s executive with his menswear line. Although the designer continues to root his aesthetic in refined tailoring, more recently his approach has included dazzling obsessive detail, veering between the avant-garde and a darkly theatrical cartoon-like element.

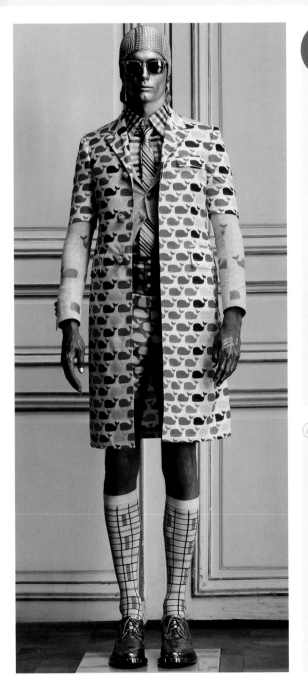

? The rise and fall of men's hemlines had never been open to much speculation until Browne designed this collection of menswear, which featured shrunken jackets and cropped trousers. Collections that appear to contain little commercial relevance when seen on the catwalk often subsequently prove to be influential, particularly when they appear in the press without the benefit of the styling that is employed on the models. Components of a collection are frequently extracted from an extreme overall look, which renders them commercially viable.

"

Maybe guys are not gonna want to wear my stuff, but they'll think that they can maybe wear something a little bit more than what they've been wearing. That's the only way things move forward.

CHAPTER THREE
PROVOCATION

Provocative dress or undress is worn for effect, often to evoke feelings of sexual excitement, as seen in Julien Macdonald's barely there dress and Beyoncé's second-skin bodysuit embellished with sequinned trompe l'oeil breasts. Designers also create garments that are designed to shock: Versace incorporated fetish fashion into the mainstream with its black leather chaps and studded leather jacket. Jeremy Scott not only employs a witty, playful aesthetic but also acts as an *agent provocateur*, evidenced in his juxtaposition of near nakedness and thigh-high boots with a shimmering leopard-print niqab.

Freda Josephine McDonald first performed as a street musician in her birthplace, St. Louis, Missouri. Married several times, she retained the surname of her second husband, Willie Baker. After two noteworthy appearances in music hall revues, she was invited to join La Revue Nègre. Josephine Baker lived the rest of her life in France, and made her final appearance on the Paris stage in her sixties.

Costume for the 'Banana Boat' song, 1941
Carmen Miranda

Pineapple-motif swimming costume, S/S 2001
Chloé

Banana-print skirt, S/S 2011
Prada

FLYING BANANA SKIRT
JOSEPHINE BAKER
1926

At the height of the Jazz Age in the mid 1920s, a group of musicians and dancers from Harlem, New York, known as La Revue Nègre, travelled to Paris with their vaudeville act. With the relatively unknown Josephine Baker as the star, La Revue Nègre dazzled the fashionable cafe society audience of the Théâtre des Champs-Elysées and caused a stir that rippled around Europe's nightclub culture. Among a compilation of acts, Josephine danced a wild and uninhibited version of the Charleston before closing the show with an erotic dance performed with her partner Joe Alex. With Baker dressed in nothing more than a feather skirt and a string of pearls, the performance propelled her to European stardom. She then starred in *La Folie du Jour* at the Folies-Bergère music hall in Paris, with an act that combined comedy and eroticism. Her nearly nude body was clad only in a costume comprising sixteen bananas strung into a skirt, a circular bra top and strands of pearls and 'slave' bracelets. Her hairstyle remained central to the look, parted deep on one side and set in smooth Marcel waves, with an oiled, flattened 'kiss curl' positioned saucily over one eyebrow. In the words of dance critic André Levinson, '[Baker is a] sinuous idol that enslaves and incites mankind.'

Baker returned to the United States in the 1950s and 1960s in several attempts to fight racism. The National Association for the Advancement of Colored People named 20 May Josephine Baker Day in her honour.

The dynamic jazz music that emerged from the American South became the soundtrack of the US and European nightclubs at the same time as the avant-garde art movement adopted the tropes and aesthetics of African indigenous art. Pablo Picasso was the first to 'discover' *l'art nègre*, and was one of a number of artists inspired by the freshness and clarity of expression that such art practices allowed.

As cultural forces hitherto treated with derision—as primitive and savage—
African American art and music were embraced by Western cultures in the
Roaring Twenties. Representing freedom from the codes of the early 20th
century, Baker was a symbol of modernity and signalled a break from the conventions of
the past, with her uninhibited style, outrageous costumes and tongue-in-cheek sexuality.

The exaggerated hourglass figure of the Playboy Bunny paradoxically arrived at a time when the fashionable female silhouette was on the cusp of change. The bullet-shaped bosom popularized by Frederick's of Hollywood was segueing into the tubular chemise of the mid 1960s, when the feminine ideal was the ingénue pre-pubescent figure. In 2005, in an attempt to revitalize the Hefner empire, Roberto Cavalli designed a trashy new version of the Bunny suit, to which he added S&M overtones.

Wynn Valdes opened the first African American-owned business on Broadway with her sister, Mary Barbour, in 1948, and was the first African American designer to open her own shop. With a signature style of form-fitting fishtail gowns, she dressed singers such as Josephine Baker, Ella Fitzgerald and Eartha Kitt.

PLAYBOY BUNNY COSTUME
ZELDA WYNN VALDES
1960

The defining feature of the Playboy Club founded by Hugh Hefner in 1960 was the women, who were chosen for their pulchritude and hourglass figures, and hired to serve drinks to an ogling clientele. Fuelling a generation of male fantasies, the Playboy Bunny outfit was officially recognized as a 'service uniform' and registered with the United States Patent and Trademark Office. Based on the tuxedo-wearing Playboy rabbit mascot, the uniform was conceived by Playboy's director of promotions, Victor Lownes, and designed by African American Zelda Wynn Valdes (1905–2001). The costume is padded out and cinched in to create a fantasy female: one well-schooled in the art of subservience and with prescribed notions of behaviour. The heavily boned satin-rayon corset is cut high on the leg to display the lower hips and low on the bodice to exhibit ample cleavage. The stiff white collar sports a black bow tie and matching cuffs fasten with cufflinks, providing an ironic facsimile of a man's tuxedo while offering a teasing sense of dress and undress. Satin rabbit ears are worn attached to a headband, and the final touch, a white cottontail, is secured to the back seam.

Baby-doll dress and bunny ears, S/S 2001
Betsey Johnson

Madonna in bunny ears, 2009
Louis Vuitton

In 1963, political activist Gloria Steinem exposed the exploitation of the underpaid waitresses in an essay titled 'A Bunny's Tale'. However, these parodies of desirable womanhood continued to inhabit the Playboy world until the more outré or sophisticated entertainments of the 1980s rendered them obsolete.

? The arrival of the monokini occurred on the cusp of the era's burgeoning acceptance of nudity, yet the garment created a prurient interest in the popular press and spawned many tawdry copies. Representing an idea rather than the reality, the monokini was a foretaste of the changing attitudes to come, which emphasized fashion for the young and nubile and made the bikini G-string that followed acceptable on public beaches.

! Gernreich's final accomplishment was the pubikini, photographed by Helmut Newton in 1985. It was intended to showcase a woman's pubic hair, which was shaped and painted bright green.

THE MONOKINI
RUDI GERNREICH
1964

Radical designer Rudi Gernreich (1922–85) first introduced the taboo-breaking monokini—a term coined by the designer—in 1964. It was designed to be worn by both men and women as part of Gernreich's drive to promulgate the notion of unisex clothing. The monokini was a natural development of the knitted maillot, which the designer had popularized in 1952, when he eliminated the complicated boned and underpinned interior construction that was then obligatory in swimwear. Predictably greeted with horror by church dignitaries, and with lukewarm reviews from the fashion press, the monokini was nevertheless a best seller for Gernreich as soon as it appeared. Cut along traditional lines, the black suit extends from the midriff to the upper thigh, with a seam at the centre front to which are attached two knitted straps that fasten at the back of the neck, bypassing and delineating the exposed breasts. The waistband is neatly turned under and hemmed, as are the edges of the leg openings, which are cut straight across the top of the thigh. Photographed by William Claxton, this image of the monokini, modelled by Gernreich's long-time muse Peggy Moffitt, entered fashion's lexicon of iconic garments that defined an era.

Using his early experience with the Lester Horton dance company, Gernreich was inspired to liberate the body from the constraints of formal clothing: he perceived the freeing of the breasts as a social statement rather than a deliberate act of provocation. In 1964, he designed the 'No Bra' bra, manufactured in a neutral-coloured jersey without padding or boning, in which breasts were no longer moulded into points but allowed to assume their natural shape.

'Pull' swimsuit, 1977
Norma Kamali

Black monokini, 2009
Andros by Sauvage

Black monokini, 2013
Victoria's Secret

One of fashion's most outstanding iconoclasts, Gernreich was born in Vienna, the son of a hosiery manufacturer. After fleeing the Nazis in the late 1930s, he settled in Los Angeles and became a US citizen in 1943. He designed his own line of clothes in Los Angeles and New York until 1951. Some years later, he opened his own company G. R. Designs Inc. which was renamed Rudi Gernreich Inc. in 1964.

The body is a legitimate dimension of human reality and can be used for a lot of things besides sex.

With no single distinctive style, the 1970s included a fashion lexicon of bad taste, from hot pants, extremely flared trousers and an unappealing palette of brown and orange, to loud shirts, legwarmers and sequinned tube tops. All these trends were brief fads, worn only by the young, and all conspired to identify the decade as one that style forgot.

HOT PANTS
1975

After the freedom of the youthquake fashions of the 1960s and the brevity of the miniskirt, hemlines plummeted to mid-thigh in the 1970s during a period of nostalgia for the flowing lines of 1930s bias-cut dresses. The longer mid-calf 'midi' skirt—officially launched in Paris in 1970—was met with some resistance by a generation that was used to short skirts and bare legs, and led directly to the adoption of 'hot pants' by an urban young who regarded the midi skirt as middle-aged. Hot pants were designed initially by contemporary practitioners, including Mary Quant, who introduced jacquard-patterned knitted short shorts with ruffle straps in 1971. Other hot pants were tailored in luxurious fabrics, such as velvet and satin, and in bright colours, such as purple and turquoise. They were worn with coloured tights or striped over-the-knee socks and many layered platform shoes. By the middle of the decade, hot pants were being customized from blue jeans. Here, the figure-hugging cut-offs are styled individually with a hand-printed star, studs, and frayed or rolled-up hems, accessorized with a Western-style buckled leather belt slung across the hips. The trend for double-denim—a 1970s casual wear staple combination—is completed by the denim shirts, worn open with a tied scarf at the neck.

Very short denim cut-offs became known as Daisy Dukes, after the female protagonist in the US cult television show *The Dukes of Hazzard* (1979–85). A movie was made in 2005, starring Jessica Simpson as Daisy.

 The fashion for hot pants introduced shorts into mainstream fashion. Contemporary short shorts are customarily denim cut-offs, often worn over black opaque tights in winter. In warmer weather, they expose a new erogenous zone: the lower buttock cheek. Short enough to expose the pocket flaps, hot pants have become a music festival uniform, popularized by influential British model Kate Moss.

Gold hot pants, 2000
Worn by Kylie Minogue

Thigh-high-cut shorts, 2011
Chanel

Barely there shorts, S/S 2012
Jason Wu

Utilizing existing garments and exploring radical ways of cutting fabric, Westwood adopted an anti-fashion stance that involved reinterpreting the function of a garment. This included repositioning the neckline and armholes, inserting gussets and using non-traditional methods of construction. Influenced by bondage paraphernalia, the designer created tartan bondage suits, incorporated found objects such as chicken bones and appropriated the safety pin as a radical statement.

Safety-pin dress, 1994
Versace

Mohair sweater,
A/W 2006/07
Junya Watanabe

Laddered sweater, 2008
Rodarte

DESTROY T-SHIRT
VIVIENNE WESTWOOD
1977

Chief architects of the punk movement Vivienne Westwood (1941–) and Malcolm McLaren promulgated a DIY ethos in fashion, whereby individuals were empowered to construct their own identity through a bricolage approach to fashion. The T-shirt is the easiest garment to customize because it is both accessible and cheap; this makes it the ideal canvas on which to express anarchic slogans such as those derived from ideas drawn from radical Situationist politics. Shirts emblazoned with 'God Save the Queen' and 'Anarchy in the UK' from Westwood's 1970s Seditionaries boutique epitomized the desire to shock and provoke. Worn by the self-styled Johnny Rotten, who was chosen by iconoclast McLaren to front the punk rock band the Sex Pistols, this T-shirt is transformed into a polemic for the punk ethos with the text 'DESTROY' emblazoned across the front. Photographed by Dennis Morris, the T-shirt was worn to promote the Virgin record label's release in 1977 of the single 'God Save the Queen', hence the collaged image of the stamp portraying the head of Queen Elizabeth II. In a deliberate act of provocation, the highly charged symbol of the swastika is overlaid with an upside-down image of Christ on the cross, thus managing to offend all aspects of the establishment.

Every time punk comes up, they think of me as a kind of trophy.

Westwood and McLaren opened a series of boutiques on London's Kings Road, including Sex in 1974 and Seditionaries in 1976. Westwood produced her first independent collection, 'Pirate', in 1981, which was an indication of the designer's future preoccupation with the cut and construction of fashions from the 17th and 18th centuries.

The punk themes of deconstruction and destruction continue to be reinterpreted by designers, in a reversal of the process in which fashions are first seen on the catwalk before being disseminated for the mass market. The 'trickle up' of ideas to the runway is exemplified by the exhibition 'Punk: Chaos to Couture,' held at New York's Metropolitan Museum of Art in 2013; it featured examples of punk's impact on haute couture and designers such as Alexander McQueen, Helmut Lang and Miuccia Prada.

Black skirt, 2008
Yohji Yamamoto

Belted sarong, S/S 2009
Etro

Kilt, 2010
Marc Jacobs

In 1984, Gaultier designed his original skirt for men. In reality it was a pair of trousers with a wrap front, and the design was inspired by a pair of Bermuda shorts by French couturier Jacques Esterel.

Gaultier's aesthetic has always been marked by a convergence of haute couture technique and influences from street style. Certain components are constant: technically adroit tailoring, trench coats, lace and corsets from the boudoir and a nautical look that includes his personal appropriation of the Breton striped top and tartan kilt. Eclectic sources of inspiration include religious iconography, an homage to Frida Kahlo, Inuit sealskins and tsarist Russia.

MALE SKIRT
JEAN PAUL GAULTIER
1993

Male dress has been bifurcated since the 16th century, but intermittent efforts have been made to render the male skirt fashionable, with little commercial success. Jean Paul Gaultier (1952–) attempted to rectify the sartorial inequality between the sexes with his 'Tatouages et Piercings' collection of 1993. Although the collection fell under the menswear designation, the presentation included both male and female models. The silk-chiffon skirt has enough associations with antique Greek dress to render it acceptable as masculine attire, particularly when it is underpinned by associations with the military kilt and worn by an athletic model. The screen-printed fabric features mythological figures, such as the Minotaur and sea serpents, against a background of ancient maps, rendered in the colours and texture of inked skin. Diffusing the disruptive visions of gender, Gaultier feels the need to put trousers underneath the skirt, thereby reinforcing the ambiguity of the image. Classical Greece meets North Africa with the jewelled collars and 'slave' bangles, so-called because of their relationship with manacles. When the collection was revisited for the designer's thirty-year retrospective in 2007, the male models were overtly androgynous, reflecting changing attitudes to men in skirts, and the tattoo-inspired patterning of the textile extended to the models' limbs.

From pioneering underwear as outerwear to popularizing the use of stretch fabrics in his signature bodysuits, Gaultier has been credited with many fashion innovations. However, it was the introduction of his haute couture collection in 1997 that established him in the fashion firmament.

Gaultier frequently introduces the subversion of gendered dressing into his menswear collections as a means of injecting novelty into male attire, first seen in 1985 in the 'Et Dieu créa l'homme' (And God Created Man) collection, a pastiche of Roger Vadim's film . . .And God Created Woman (1956). However, skirts for men continue to be marginal to mainstream fashion, with the exception of variations of the kilt.

? Macdonald's reputation as the go-to label for career-enhancing dresses was consolidated by the appearance of Joely Richardson at a film premiere in 2000, when she wore the designer's sequinned gold micro-dress, cut to reveal the buttocks and held in place with transparent thread. Few designers would dare to bare like Macdonald, and in pushing the limits of acceptable nudity on the red carpet he is unparalleled.

**BARELY THERE DRESS
JULIEN MACDONALD
1999**

Chief exponent of the über-glamorous nearly nude dress, Julien Macdonald (1971–) eschews discreet good taste and understated elegance for the showstopping effect of glitter and sparkle, which he uses to provide the merest cover for the naked body beneath. The designer's technical wizardry with the potential of the knitted stitch has been paramount to his global success. His instantly recognizable signature cobweb dresses appear in some form or another in every collection; for 1999, they are off-the-shoulder or one-shouldered figure-enhancing slips of dresses, cropped to the crotch and with more holes than substance, all finished with a metallic shimmer. Macdonald deploys his signature skin-coloured base in transparent stretch fabric in this barely there dress to support short curved lengths of metallic sticks, which strategically cluster more thickly over the hips and breasts and give the appearance of iron filings attracted to a magnet. Elsewhere in the collection, an asymmetrical knit mesh dress is fringed to the knee, and outsize paillettes are invisibly strung together to form a mid-calf dress. A full-skirted, ankle-length gown of knitted ribbons provides an element of couture elegance.

 Exemplifying the edict that 'more is more' in terms of luxury embellishment, Macdonald sent down the runway in 2001 the most expensive dress he could devise. He attached a corsage embellished with more than one thousand hand-cut diamonds on the shoulder of a black knitted minidress; it was worth more than a million pounds and was designed in collaboration with diamond company De Beers.

 Karl Lagerfeld spotted Macdonald's risqué knits during his postgraduate show in 1996, and commissioned him to produce knitwear for Chanel. The following year, Macdonald launched his own label, and from 2001 to 2004 he was chief designer at the couture house Givenchy. In 2013, he opened an atelier to service celebrities, such as Heidi Klum, who demand a bespoke experience for their high-profile activities.

 Lace minidress,
A/W 1997/98
Dior Haute Couture

Fluoro fringed minidress,
S/S 2011
Mark Fast

Lace gown, A/W 2013/14
Armani Privé Couture

 In June 2006, the Welsh designer was awarded the rank of Officer of the Order of the British Empire in the Queen's Birthday Honours list for his services to the fashion industry.

McQueen's sartorial daring resulted in widespread attention and critical acclaim. The designer won the Council of Fashion Designers of America International Designer of the Year Award in 2003, the same year that he was made a Commander of the British Empire for his services to the fashion industry. In 2010, the British Fashion Council posthumously honoured him for Outstanding Achievement in Fashion Design with the rider: he had 'an exceptional impact on global fashion.'

Uomo jeans, 2012
Christian Dior

Premium denim brand,
A/W 2013/14
J. Brand

BUMSTER JEANS
ALEXANDER McQUEEN
2000

From their inception in 1993 until well into the 21st century, the infamous bumster trousers radically changed the proportions of the trouser. The design was introduced by Alexander McQueen (1969–2010) in his autumn/winter collection 1993/94, and it reappeared frequently in the seasons that followed. However, the design received little attention until it featured in the 'Highland Rape' collection of autumn/winter 1995/96, which was the first of McQueen's shows to be staged under the aegis of the British Fashion Council at London Fashion Week. The flat-fronted bumster trousers are cut with McQueen's customary surgical precision, designed to sit low on the hip with an abbreviated rise, visually elongating the torso and shortening the leg. Here, the more relaxed fit and generous cut of the jeans in 2000 renders the short crotch less overtly sexual, but the distressed denim proffers a generous glimpse of bum cleavage, previously the prerogative of builders. By 2000, deliberately patched and ripped jeans, worn low on the hips, had hit the high street, lessening their impact. A low rise demands a cropped top, and the purple cotton turtle-neck sweater in oversized garter stitch stops just short of the waist. The back of the garment consists of loops of yarn falling from the loose cowl of the collar.

The Alexander McQueen collections include women's ready-to-wear, men's ready-to-wear, accessories, eyewear and two scents: Kingdom launched in 2003 and My Queen in 2005.

The 'rise' of any trouser is determined by the distance between the crotch and the waist, and this usually measures approximately 30 centimetres (12 in.). In the low-rise version, the zip is often only 5 or 6 centimetres (2 or 3 in.) in length. This style can be differentiated from the oversized jeans worn by hip-hop stars, which also drop to the hip bone or below.

? Inspired by McQueen's bumsters, the low-rise jean is ubiquitous in the 21st century for both men and women. Pop star Britney Spears is most credited with popularizing the fashion in the United States after she started to wear low-rise trousers in 2000; hers stopped just short of her pubic bone. The low-rise trouser is also the contemporary norm for the tailored trouser, particularly in conjunction with the skinny leg. Although attempts are often made to place the waistband of the trouser on the natural line, these trends are usually short-lived.

[With bumsters] I wanted to elongate the body, not just show the bum. To me that part of the body—not so much the buttocks but the bottom of the spine—that's the most erotic part of anyone's body.

Demeulemeester was one of the chief protagonists of deconstruction in fashion. She has since honed her design signature of androgynous dressing through tailoring, and for women has introduced a number of wrapping and draping techniques. The emphasis is on asymmetrical cuts, layering and a multiplicity of textures, including felted wool, velvet and leather, offset with white linen and cotton.

POETIC ANDROGYNY
ANN DEMEULEMEESTER
2009

An ode to the 'quintessential Ann Demeulemeester man,' according to Erik Madigan Heck, founder of *Nomenus Quarterly* magazine, the editorial draws on the archives of Belgian designer Ann Demeulemeester (1959–). The retrospective from 1996 to 2009 represents Demeulemeester's male archetype, one of poetic androgyny, mediated through impeccable, if fragmented, tailoring and a palette limited to black and white. This could be read as a coherent expression of the counterpoint duality at the heart of the designer's inspiration and an adoption of singer-songwriter Patti Smith as monochrome muse. Smith and photographer Robert Mapplethorpe formed an edgy duet of sound and

Frock coat, A/W 2006/07
Raf Simons

Collarless jacket and shirt,
A/W 2009/10
Lucas Ossendrijver for Lanvin

One of the Antwerp Six
—a group of pioneering
designers who studied at
Antwerp's Royal Academy of
Fine Arts and also included
Dries Van Noten and
Walter Van Beirendonck—
Demeulemeester founded
her eponymous label in
1985. The designer showed
her first collection in Paris
in 1992.

vision that is recalled by Demeulemeester's retrospective echoing of Smith's lyric: 'About a boy, beyond it all.' The garments have a faded, well-used quality, in keeping with the designer's earlier preoccupation with deconstruction, in which the traditional means of constructing and finishing clothing is discarded in favour of reassembling pieces, exposing seams and leaving edges unfinished. The complicated layering and distressed fabrics have intimations of a crew of gold prospectors from the Klondike—a nuanced acknowledgement of social marginalism inferred by a dishevelled silhouette with emphasis on variations of the waistcoat, collarless shirts, a battered fedora and ecru long johns. A shrunken sweater is worn over wide-legged shorts and elements of sartorial savvy are seen in the palely bound blazer. The defining piece of the collection—a crimped collar on a waistcoat—reappears on the deep shawl collar of a leather jacket cropped at the waist.

? Without allure
or coquetry,
Demeulemeester
proffers an offhand
romanticism with a gothic
edge, an aesthetic that is
not subject to the extreme
vagaries of fashion. The
designer's collections for
men and women are virtually
interchangeable—in palette,
texture and silhouette—a
concept that was shared by
fellow Belgian Raf Simons at
Jil Sander and can be seen
in collections by Colombian
designer Haider Ackermann.

Gupta emblazons a variety of images with sequinned graphics, and all are hand-embellished in his artisan workshops in India. His inspiration is diverse, ranging from protective clothing and African fabrics, to Nike's Swoosh and Disney's cartoon characters. The designer is less concerned with fit and structure than surface decoration: even an excursion into denim staples, such as boyfriend jeans, is lavishly embellished with all-over sequins in denim blue.

Sequins, glamour, sportswear and more sequins.

ASHISH GUPTA

CUT-OUT DRESS
ASHISH
2010

London-based designer Ashish Gupta (1973–) does not limit his hand-sequinned patterning to evening wear; it is utilized to convey his rapid turnover of ideas in a collection that includes Hawaiian print shirts, images of parrots and flamingos, and cityscapes of New York and Paris, all in rainbow-hued sequins. These are inspired by vintage postcards and appear alongside garments emblazoned with peace signs and text. The glittering images are worked into sporty separates in an acknowledgement of the 1980s, with oversized T-shirts and T-shirt dresses worn over loosely gathered peg-top trousers. The 1980s was also an era in which the body-con dress emerged, epitomized by designers such as Versace and Azzedine Alaïa. This version is more flesh than dress. With a sporty vest top with narrow wide-spaced straps and cropped to mid-thigh, the sequinned dress features cut-outs that replicate the curve of the neckline, forming a pleasing symmetry. These appear at the midriff, hips and thighs, creating a central panel of intense, shimmering colour and superimposing an hourglass shape. The dress is anchored at the hips, reducing the potential for red-carpet embarrassment, by a low-slung bumbag in leather, studded with spikes. On the catwalk, the sportswear vibe infiltrates the night-time glamour with black visors and buckled gold lamé wedges.

Amorphous dress, 1977
Swanky Modes

White cut-out gown,
A/W 2010/11
Versace

Draped cut-out gown,
A/W 2011/12
Halston

After graduating in 2000, Gupta first showed his signature embroidered clothes on the catwalk within the schedule of London Fashion Week in 2003. He received NEWGEN sponsorship on three occasions, and the label has also successfully collaborated with British high-street retailer Topshop.

Cut-outs in dresses first appeared in the 1960s, when designers such as John Bates introduced them to A-line shift dresses, albeit with the insertion of a mesh or transparent panel of fabric. The innovation of new fibres and technology has enabled designers to enhance fit without gaping, thereby solving the problem that always occurs when the area that is cut out is greater than the garment. Providing minimal coverage and maximum exposure, dresses with cut-outs are red-carpet favourites, worn by celebrities who are keen to show off their toned bodies.

? A number of artists have drawn on visceral or corporeal imagery to explore the borderlines of the body. The initial shock and revulsion of such 'carnal art' provokes disgust, but Gaga's appropriation of raw meat as a suitable medium for a show costume attracted both incredulity and derision. The animal rights organization PETA released the statement, 'Wearing a dress made from cuts of dead cows is offensive enough to bring comment, but someone should whisper in her ear that more people are upset by butchery than are impressed by it.'

"

If we don't stand up for what we believe in and if we don't fight for our rights pretty soon we're going to have as much rights as the meat on our bones.

LADY GAGA

MEAT DRESS
FRANC FERNANDEZ
2010

Fashion designers draw on the visual symbols of the memento mori tradition, appropriating images of death such as skulls, human hair and bones to convey the frailty of life and the potential for decay. These devices are often used to highlight the contrast between the inevitability of death and the lively, artificial world re-created on the catwalk or stage. By explicitly referencing death with a costume that incorporated raw beef, Lady Gaga was in direct opposition to the traditions of the glamorous show costumes worn by her contemporaries. In 2010, she arrived at the MTV Video Music Awards wearing an Alexander McQueen dress and changed into a Giorgio Armani evening gown before donning her final outfit of the evening for her acceptance of the Video of the Year trophy for 'Bad Romance'. Created by Argentinian designer Franc Fernandez and styled by Nicola Formichetti, the meat dress was constructed from flank steak and was accessorized with matching boots, lashed to Gaga's feet with butcher's string. After the ceremony, the dress was archived, and it subsequently went on display in 2011 at the Rock and Roll Hall of Fame after being preserved by taxidermist Sergio Vigilato, who treated the dress with bleach, formaldehyde and detergent to kill any bacteria.

The wet and gleaming raw meat is disturbingly suggestive of flayed flesh, a connotation that will not have escaped Lady Gaga when she was breaking powerful taboos concerned with putrification, the subsequent smells and the potential danger to health. Blurring the lines between her own flesh and that of the dress, Gaga draws a correlation between wearing meat and being treated like meat in her determination not to be a victim of the machinations of the pop industry.

Vanitas: Flesh Dress for an Albino Anorectic, 1987
Jana Sterbak

Bodysuit with arteries and blood vessels, A/W 1998/99
Olivier Theyskens

In a mash-up of David Bowie, Madonna and Freddie Mercury (Gaga has attributed the inspiration for her name to the 1984 Queen song 'Radio Ga Ga'), the postmodern diva Lady Gaga continually seeks new ways to reinvent herself, discarding each incarnation like an outworn skin to take on a fresh persona with every new appearance.

The meat dress was satirized in *The Simpsons* episode 'Lisa Goes Gaga' (2012), in which Homer takes pieces of meat from Lady Gaga's dress (while it is still being worn), then cooks and eats them.

Mastache studied fine art before enrolling at the Advanced School of Design, Textiles and Fashion of Galicia. In 2008, she won first prize at the Tesoira Galician competition for new fashion designers, and the following year she was awarded the first prize for the best end of university collection. During 2009, the avant-garde designer worked as an intern at the Spanish womenswear brand D-due, before launching her own eponymous label.

PRINTED WOOL JACKET AND TOTEM HAT
ISABEL MASTACHE
2010

A Dada mash-up of prosthetic arms, trousers deftly tailored to boast a matching set of cloth penis and scrotum and a man in a giant knitted duck outfit with turned heels for decoration appears in a fun-fixated autumn/winter menswear collection by Spanish-born designer Isabel Mastache (1984–). The designer determinedly manifests her playful, eclectic aesthetic in a continuous montage of surreal juxtapositions. A tutu made from gloves is forced into three-way cohabitation with a striped weightlifter vest and a paper party hat; a pinstripe gullet is revealed in the opening of a faux all-in-one; and a three-sleeved jacket features a red bleeding heart appliquéd aptly to the breast pocket. Potential retail feasibility erupts with a shrunken duffel coat worn with peg-top trousers, a vertically striped blazer and this single-breasted jacket, cut along conventional lines and constructed from felted wool. Worn over a starred and printed T-shirt, it is adorned with Egyptian patterning—lapis-lazuli tones and palmate gold scrolling—which is echoed in the face-framing headgear, something like a lotus plant climbing a totem pole, with a swatch of Guatemalan bright tapestry to provide a clash of cultures. A preppy moment of relative respite is afforded by loosely fitting trews in a Black Watch tartan, which are cropped at the ankle.

> The fashion world can be a strange, strange place, but designer Isabel Mastache upped the weirdness ante.
>
> THE HUFFINGTON POST

Bucket hat, A/W 2013/14
Fashion East Menswear

Oversized knitted hat, A/W 2013/14
Sibling

Pom-pom balaclava, A/W 2013/14 William Richard Green/The North Circular

Showing as part of Cibeles Madrid Fashion Week 2010, Mastache introduced a capricious idiosyncrasy to the trope of traditional menswear. She continues to effect this by expropriating fragments of other cultures and subverting the conventional jacket and trouser combination with bold print and texture.

Formal hats such as the fedora, trilby, bowler and summer panama are more usually known for their associations with mid 20th-century film stars, such as Humphrey Bogart, or the city gent. By introducing a decorative cone-shaped hat of towering proportions into contemporary menswear, Mastache is harking back to the various eras when male headgear symbolized political status and wealth or signified an occupation, such as a sailor. In this case, the role would be the Shakespearean fool or Punchinello from the commedia dell'arte, complete with false beard.

The potential of laser cutting, originally an industrial manufacturing application, was first realized by fashion designers in the 21st century. Since then, it has been used to create effects that would otherwise have involved time-consuming craft practices, such as pierced leather and handmade lace. The process hinges upon the delivery of a highly focused, intensified blade of light to the material to be cut or engraved.

LASER-CUT BACK DRESS
VILSBØL DE ARCE
2010

Titled 'Anatomy', the autumn/winter 2010/11 collection by Danish design duo Vilsbøl de Arce was shown within an installation designed as a ribcage, with striated wooden bands spiralling around the runway. Restricted to a palette of black and white, the collection explores the infrastructure of the human body, abstracting anatomical elements, such as the ribcage and spine, to superimpose a second silhouette. The designers employ techniques of padding, pleating, draping and laser cutting to transform the organic shapes into futuristic silhouettes. A series of body-con dresses features areas, such as the small of the back, the upper arms or the hips, that have been quilted and padded to emulate the movement of the muscles beneath the skin. High-waisted black jersey trousers incorporate the same technique, spiralling around the legs in a manner similar to the protective clothing worn for fencing, and a white leather cape includes a grown-on gorget at the back of the neck. A white leather dress is laser cut into fronds that fall into wings at the shoulder, while the back of a black dress is slashed into ribbons to form ribs that fall away each side of the centre back zip. Elsewhere, cut close to the body, the soft leather billows out to form dolman sleeves that commence at the waist.

Following an approach that is characterized by minimal decoration and is limited to a palette of black and white, with the occasional shot of vibrant colour, Vilsbøl de Arce's work is sculptural in its intensity. The designers are preoccupied with redefining the human figure: treating the body as an armature on which extraneous surfaces can be built, and playing with volume and proportion by adding emphasis to various parts of the body through padding, braiding, quilting and geometric cutting techniques.

Black cocktail dress, 2010
Valentino

Laser-cut gown, 2011
Marchesa

Laser-cut swan gown, 2012
Giles

After graduating in 2002 from the Copenhagen Academy of Fashion and Design, Prisca Vilsbøl and Pia de Arce joined forces to create the label Vilsbøl de Arce. They alternate between art projects and fashion collections, with little distinction made between the two. Vilsbøl de Arce won the Design Talent of the Year at the 2010 Danish Fashion Awards.

Our philosophy is to maintain a certain exploration and adventure. . .keeping to the belief that anything is possible.

FUR BIKINI
JEREMY SCOTT
2011

With an aesthetic firmly rooted in Americana—cartoon superhero motifs and parodies of consumerism proliferate—Scott might be considered Los Angeles's fashion outsider. However, as the sole owner of his label, the designer has collaborated successfully with companies such as Swatch and Longchamp as well as Adidas, for whom he designed wing high-tops, thus achieving commercial appeal without forsaking his signature cartoon-inspired playful style.

Leopard-print bikini, 1963
Worn by Jayne Mansfield

Fur bikini, 1966
Worn by Raquel Welch

Partly inspired by Alicia Silverstone's character in the hyper-fashion world of Amy Heckerling's film *Clueless* (1995), Jeremy Scott (1976–) provides perfect Barbie-doll style for the legions of adherents to his pop fashion aesthetic. Combining cropped bright orange shearling jackets with furry angora dresses and silver lamé hot pants, the collection embodies a Lolita-esque quality, emphasized by neon-bright colours, the high-tied bunches of the model's fluorescent hair and her dramatic doll-like painted lashes. The designer summons up a sugar-pink vision of girlie sparkles, with a classically detailed trench coat reworked in transparent plastic. The single-breasted raincoat has wide revers and an upturned collar, and it is cinched in at the waist with a wide, transparent belt. The princess-line seams, running from shoulder to hem, add fit and flare to the silhouette, resulting in a mid-thigh skater skirt. The coat hem, the edges of the revers and the cuffs are all sprinkled with Swarovski crystals. A pink fur bikini is worn beneath the coat: the halter-neck top just manages to enclose a pneumatic bosom and the bikini bottoms are tied low on the hips. Providing grist for the shoe fetishist, pink fur subverts the ingénue quality of the matching strapped and high-heeled Mary Janes.

One of Scott's closest collaborators is legendary Parisian stylist Carlyne Cerf de Dudzeele, who styled numerous *Vogue* covers; she first worked with Scott on his autumn/winter 2013/14 show.

Appealing to an array of well-known clients, including Katy Perry and Britney Spears, Scott's approach to womenswear—as short and as tight as possible—relies on the same components throughout all his collections. These include second-skin hot pants, crop tops, barely there tank dresses and über-fitted minis, all in neon-bright colours and incorporating spandex.

? Beneath the transparent plastic raincoat, Scott seemingly channels Britain's answer to Marilyn Monroe, pop culture siren Diana Dors, with the inclusion of a pink fur bikini. Dors is mostly remembered for her impressive embonpoint and the press coup of sporting a mink bikini during the Venice Film Festival in 1955, an image of which appeared in the media worldwide. The bikini has been a seaside staple since the 1960s, but it has always been the go-to outfit for the pin-up photographic shoot, in which maximum exposure is a prerequisite and practicality is not an issue.

Red-carpet gowns don't float my boat. There are enough boring clothes in the world.

? Fetishes are usually associated with sexual fantasies, with sexual arousal contingent on the presence of particular objects, such as shoes, or fabrics, including latex and leather. Often associated with sadomasochism, fetishism moved from the marginal youth subculture of punk, which appropriated fetish clothing, to mainstream fashion in the 1990s, when Versace launched its bondage collection in 1992. Since then, the recurring theme of fetish in fashion has become more extreme, moving from the fringes of the sexual subculture to the catwalk.

> *I scream for quality and fantasy, but I understand if these straps of leather are not to everyone's liking. I don't mind if people say I'm vulgar.*
> GIANNI VERSACE

LEATHER JACKET AND CHAPS
VERSACE
2012

In a collection of vibrantly patterned jumpsuits and slick mohair suiting, Donatella Versace (1955–) harks back to the 1990s and the heyday of fetish fashion for a souped-up version of cowboy style, combined with brooding Marlon Brando machismo. The black leather motorcycle jacket worn by the anti-hero of the film *The Wild One* (1953) came to signify intransigent rebellion and uncompromising masculinity, attitudes reinforced in *Rebel Without a Cause* (1955) by movie bad boy James Dean, whose styling featured his characteristic slicked-back quiff and hollow-eyed pallor. Here the Perfecto-style jacket, originally designed by Irving Schott in 1928, is cut close to the body with the double-faced zippered opening delineated by rows of studs, which describe the wide revers and shoulder line, as well as mark the horizontal slant of the zipped-up pockets. The jacket is worn over another fashion staple of the gym-honed look: a fine black fitted T-shirt. In order to provide emphasis on the crotch, the denim jeans are overlaid with a facsimile of chaps: the loose strapped-on protective trousers worn by free-ranging, hard-riding cowboys. The chaps are tucked into heavy-duty strapped and buckled motorcycle boots. Black fingerless gloves are festooned with metal chains.

Founded in 1978 by Gianni Versace (1946–97), the fashion house is forever associated with the high-voltage, decadent glamour of the 1990s, when vibrantly coloured, Baroque patterning and body-con leather provided an exuberant contrast to nihilistic, down-and-dirty grunge fashion. Previously the director of the more youthful and edgier Versus line, Gianni's sister and long-term muse Donatella Versace assumed the creative direction of the house in 1997.

Bondage suit, 1976
Vivienne Westwood

Leather jacket, bondage trousers, S/S 2011
John Galliano

Donatella Versace continues to imbue the house with skin-baring collections for the body beautiful. Here, the designer combines the cowboy and the cop in a subconscious parody of the disco group Village People, formed in 1977, which featured gay US cultural stereotypes including the construction worker, the cowboy and the GI.

Versace is credited with using commercial print faces such as Christy Turlington, Cindy Crawford and Linda Evangelista on the runway, giving rise to the term 'supermodel' in 1991.

The sequinned trompe l'oeil bodysuit fulfils the provocative, glamorous and eye-catching criteria required by a musical diva of worldwide renown. Such a garment must carry out a number of functions: firstly, it must provide a focal point on the stage that can be seen from a distance, and secondly, it must create a strong enough image to attract publicity outside of the arena in the print media. Finally, and most importantly, the garment has to withstand the erotic posturings and rigours of the singer's stage performance.

> *I don't wanna be a hot girl. I wanna be iconic.*
> BEYONCÉ

TROMPE L'OEIL COSTUME
PHILLIPE AND DAVID BLOND
2013

Beyoncé is one of the most recognized icons of contemporary pop music, and the common theme throughout her career has been the wearing of garments that showcase her renowned body shape. An archetype of US showgirl glamour, the singer wears a sequinned leotard embellished with trompe l'oeil breasts and abdominal muscles, created by Phillipe and David Blond of design house The Blonds for 'The Mrs. Carter Show' world tour. Designed to be worn on the stage of a vast stadium, this anatomically correct depiction of the singer's body was initially hand painted on Beyoncé to ensure the correct shading, and the garment was then hand embellished with approximately thirty thousand Swarovski crystals in order to provide the shimmering trompe l'oeil effect. The high-cut leg line, designed to lengthen the legs, is accented by a fringe to emphasize the much-lauded and energetic gyrations of the singer. Polish-born artist Tamara de Lempicka, who found fame in the 1920s and 1930s with her exotic and glamorous portraits of powerful women in the style of Art Deco, has been cited as a direct influence on the costume, but the disco glamour epitomized by US pop diva Diana Ross is also very much in evidence.

Trompe l'oeil dress,
A/W 1983/84
Geoffrey Beene

Corset with beaded fringe
and sequins for Madonna,
1990
Jean Paul Gaultier

Jewelled tutu for Katy Perry,
2011
Giorgio Armani

Based in New York, design duo Phillipe and David Blond are known for creating extravagant corset-based costumes for pop luminaries such as Rihanna and Beyoncé—both of whom share the same glamorous and provocative aesthetic. The designers are the latest in a long line of collaborators with whom Beyoncé and her stylist mother, Tina Knowles, have worked.

Trompe l'oeil (meaning trick of the eye) is the playful conceit of adorning flat surfaces with a two-dimensional design to mimic a three-dimensional object; it was first seen in 20th-century fashion in the designs of Paris-based couturière Elsa Schiaparelli. For Beyoncé, the technique provides an acceptable and effective way of showcasing the singer's body in graphic detail without revealing actual flesh.

The catsuit was first worn by Diana Rigg as Emma Peel, the kick-ass heroine of the cult British television show *The Avengers* (1961–69); this was followed by the feline-inspired garb sported by various Catwomen in the *Batman* film franchise. The all-in-one remains the go-to garment for maximum impact on the street, screen or stage, worn by pop icons such as Kylie Minogue in her '2 Hearts' video in 2007.

CATSUIT
PAM HOGG
2013

With a collection ironically titled 'The Emperor's New Clothes', after a morality tale about the folly of the desire to be fashionable written by Hans Christian Andersen and published in c. 1837, Scottish-born punk rebel Pam Hogg asserts her distance from the activities of the mainstream catwalk. Renowned for her skintight bodysuits since her days creating distinctive club wear in the 1980s and 1990s, the self-taught designer brings a combination of sporty streamlining and overt sensuality to her collection via her use of materials. These include a glossy scarlet stretch PVC interspersed with flesh-exposing sheer net. The plastic is slashed to the pubic bone and just bypasses the nipples, creating a precise wide 'V' shape, and it is cut again from the waist to just above the knee, where it is shaped to give the impression of a pair of stockings and suspenders. Dissected by a centre front seam, and again with two shaping side seams that closely adhere to the contours of the body, the catsuit is doubly seamed at the shoulders, thereby creating a raglan sleeve with a rounded shoulder pad. The tight-fitting PVC cuffs are matched to the high, ruched collar. Disregarding the millinery conventions of wearability and face-flattering appeal, the model balances an outsize rectangular box in matching scarlet PVC at the front of her head.

The dynamic London club scene of the 1980s fuelled Hogg's rebellious attitude to fashion and instigated a personal cross-fertilization of fashion, music and performance art that remains intrinsic to her output. She spent the early 1990s in a band called Doll, who supported Debbie Harry; later in the decade, she worked on films. Throughout her career, the designer has chosen to create her collections with a minimal amount of assistance. She continues to maintain a hands-on approach and still constructs some garments by hand.

Red rubber catsuit, 2012
Atsuko Kudo

Black catsuit,
A/W 2013/14
Ralph Lauren

Hogg studied printed textiles at the Glasgow School of Art and London's Royal College of Art. She launched her first fashion collection in 1981, and was one of the new wave of emerging British design talents that put London on the fashion map for radical ideas and innovation.

It's the roulette wheel. . . when the wheel stops turning and the ball drops, they fuse and a collection emerges.

? By introducing a cross between a niqab and a full-length burka into the collection (the former is a veil that covers the face, whereas a burka covers the whole body from the top of the head to the toe), Scott is not so much making a political statement as having fun, breaking various taboos based on religious iconography and costume. The wearing of the face veil predates its adoption by Islam, but it has since become a garment fraught with political controversy, particularly when worn in secular situations.

"

I'm not going anywhere. People don't want quiet fashion from me. They want the whole nine yards.

LEOPARD-PRINT NIQAB
JEREMY SCOTT
2013

Moving between the implicit sexuality of the see-through mesh dress and the face-covering niqab, Jeremy Scott (1976–) treads his customary fine line between provocation, commerciality and outrageous bad taste. Citing the Arab Spring of 2011 as his inspiration, the designer forsakes his signature playful pop-influenced aesthetic for a collection that includes machine-gun prints on silk, all-in-ones for men and miniature metal replica rifles pinned to women's dresses. The seemingly chaotic mix of pattern, texture and silhouette, which includes mock-croc hot pants and metal mesh chain-mail dresses, also features this black and gold lamé niqab in outsize abstract leopard print. The semi-transparent devoré fabric fleetingly reveals the torso beneath, partially obscuring the upper part of the body, falling to the waist at the front and floating to the ground at the back; it also has a rectangular unpatterned piece over the eyes. The micro-mini black mesh skirt shows just beneath the veil and reveals the model's underwear. Over-the-knee boots in the same gleaming mock croc as the hat emphasize the upper thigh and feature a lethal-looking metallic toecap. Every look is accessorized with a structured cap with a flat visor and full crown, designed in collaboration with New Era.

Self-styled 'style maker' and the antithesis of the red-carpet designer, Scott remains preoccupied with the dressing-up days of the 1980s and 1990s, when raves and club culture were the vehicles for anti-establishment fashion. With obsessively loyal fans, Scott challenges fashion preconceptions, yet retains a sound commercial eye for the appeal of kitsch.

West Coast-based designer Scott is a US version of a fashion 'bad boy', on a par with the early days of witty Italian designer Franco Moschino, and far removed from the 'model-off-duty' aesthetic of his slicker East Coast counterparts. In 1992, Scott moved to New York to study fashion design at the Pratt Institute in Brooklyn before moving in 1996 to Paris, where he launched his own catwalk collection the following year. He subsequently showed in New York, London, Los Angeles and Moscow.

Burka, 1996
Hussein Chalayan

Printed niqab,
A/W 2014
Cavalera

Scott was appointed creative director of Italian fashion house Moschino in 2013 and showed his first collection in Milan the following year. He continues to head up his own label.

CHAPTER FOUR
VOLUME

Numerous designers eschew the traditional hourglass shape for women that has been regarded as a paradigm of feminine beauty at various times in the fashion cycle. The female figure is exaggerated by Charles James's four-leaf-clover gown, which reintroduces the corseted figure, and diffused by Rudi Gernreich's unisex kaftans, which accommodate the silhouette of an ageing body. The traditional upturned triangle of the male silhouette is also subverted, with the influential loose-fitting zoot suit and the iconic big suit worn by David Byrne, frontman of new wave band Talking Heads.

The masculine silhouette of the upturned triangle has been evident in men's tailoring since the 1930s. The zoot suit not only exaggerated this, but also, in a less extreme version, laid down the template for menswear for the next two decades. The drape suit was a more conservative version of the zoot suit and featured a shorter jacket with enhanced production values. The shape of the zoot suit jacket was also appropriated by the neo-Edwardian youth subculture known as Teddy boys in post-war London, who transposed the cut, in vibrant colours, and wore it with drainpipe trousers.

ZOOT SUIT
1943

Wearing the zoot suit was an act of sartorial rebellion and a powerful symbol of subversion, originating in the mid to late 1930s in the African American communities of Gainesville, Georgia; Chicago, Illinois; and the Harlem neighbourhood in New York City. With its stylistic origins in the Edwardian male fashions of the early 20th century, exemplified in the drape of the jacket and the nipped-in waist, the zoot suit exaggerated certain details: for example, the width of the shoulders was increased with padding, resulting in additional bulk to the chest that then tapered to the waist. On the right, the single-breasted jacket falls almost to the knee and has a three-button fastening and extended lapels, over which the long, pointed collars of the shirt are spread. The sleeves, gathered into a deep sleeve head, bear none of the details usually found in men's tailoring. The trousers are pegged into a high waist with excessive fullness at the knee before tapering at the ankle into a cuffed hem, which falls over the two-tone correspondent wingtips. A wide-brimmed fedora is worn on the back of the head with a relaxed insouciance. Zoot suit wearers often added a watch chain dangling from the belt to the knee or below, then back to a side pocket. Commonly, fabrics were in eye-catching colours, in checks and stripes or light-coloured cotton.

'Zoot' was used as a term of approval to describe anything 'cool'. Marginalized by race and culture, African Americans who wore zoot suits came to be associated with everything 'hip', epitomized by jazz artist Cab Calloway in the 1940s. Jazz was a unifying force, and wherever the US troops were stationed, the zoot suit became fashionable. In Europe, it was associated with the wartime 'spiv' and influenced the cut of the demob suit, given to ex-service men for civilian life.

Wearers of the zoot suit were deemed unpatriotic and were lambasted for excessive use of fabric at a time of clothing rationing, which led to the Zoot Suit Riots of 1943 in Los Angeles.

African Americans and Latinos challenged the racial barriers in place in the early to mid 20th century. Worn by an underprivileged urban class who defied segregation, the zoot suit came to represent a change in social and geographical boundaries as many black Americans migrated to the cities.

Teddy-boy suit, 1972
Hardy Amies

Pastel silk suits, 1982
Antony Price for Duran Duran

?

Adrian was renowned for dressing a new breed of strong Hollywood heroines, including Norma Shearer and Barbara Stanwyck, but his most enduring association was with Joan Crawford, dressing her on twenty-eight films. He designed Crawford's signature outfits, which featured large shoulder pads and an indented waist, thus setting a trend for the archetypal 1940s silhouette. The simplicity of the designer's draped clothing heralded the pared-down minimalism that came to represent a unique American look, epitomized by later designers such as James Galanos and Halston.

"

Adrian arranged abstract shapes of fabric in juxtapositions of line and colour as deftly as if they were painted with a brush.

JAN GLIER REEDER, CURATOR

Jersey kaftan dress, 1969
Charles Kleibacker

Silk jersey evening gown, 1970
James Galanos

HOSTESS GOWN
ADRIAN
1947

Instrumental in bringing Parisian couture via the medium of film to a mass audience, Gilbert Adrian (1903–59) popularized the fluid lines of the bias-cut evening gown, previously the provenance of French couturière Madeleine Vionnet. His designs for the stars were hugely influential on the fashion industry, and as a result he left his post as chief designer at Metro-Goldwyn-Mayer in 1941 to open his eponymous outlet in Los Angeles, selling both ready-to-wear and custom-made clothes. Adrian brought to the ready-to-wear industry contemporary dressing that not only included urban tailoring for the professional woman but also utilized his mastery of cut for evening wear, seen here in the jersey hostess gown, to be worn when entertaining at home. It represents the more relaxed easy-to-wear evening dress that was typical of the era. Cut with all the finesse of its European counterparts, the gown flows from a high waist to form a train, with a voluminous cape cut in one with the shoulder.

Adrian designed costumes for the all-female cast of *The Women* (1939), one of the first films to include a fashion parade in the storyline.

Adrian was head costume designer for Cecil B. DeMille's independent film studio before moving with him to Metro-Goldwyn-Mayer in 1928. There he designed costumes for screen luminaries such as Greta Garbo and Katharine Hepburn.

One of the few US couturiers to rank alongside the couture houses of Europe, such as Balenciaga and Dior, James became renowned and celebrated for the spectacularly engineered evening wear that he produced between 1947 and 1954. The New York-based couturier created only a small body of work—fewer than one thousand garments over the nearly fifty years of his career—due in part to his meticulous and time-consuming working methods, which depended on his obsessive pursuit of perfection. James won the Coty American Fashion Critics' Award twice, once in 1950 and again in 1954, for his 'great mystery of colour and artistry of draping'.

FOUR-LEAF-CLOVER GOWN
CHARLES JAMES
1953

US couturier Charles James (1906–78) achieved cult status with his engineered gowns commissioned for the grandest of social occasions. With no formal fashion training, James developed an approach to design that defied the conventions of dressmaking and was based on mathematical concepts, seen here in the four-leaf-clover gown that was first made for a client, Austine Hearst, to wear to the Eisenhower Inaugural Ball in 1953. James was so late finishing the dress that Hearst wore it instead to the Coronation Ball of Queen Elizabeth II. The gown, considered to be the designer's 'thesis', was inspired by the 1860s silhouette and the cage crinoline. It consists of four layers: an inner taffeta slip, a structured under petticoat, a matching petticoat flare and an overdress. The unique quatrefoil silhouette is constructed from thirty pattern pieces, twenty-eight of which are cut in duplicate, the remaining two singly. The asymmetrical bodice, made from ivory duchesse satin, has an infrastructure of buckram, horsehair and covered wire, and is lined in cotton flannel. It was designed to support the voluminous and undulating overskirt, which was engineered to rest on the hips and thereby distribute its great weight.

Maria-Luisa gown, S/S 1998
John Galliano

Infanta gown, A/W 2004/05
Ralph Rucci

Propaganda gown,
A/W 2005/06
Vivienne Westwood

Widely regarded as the United States' greatest couturier, British-born James began his fashion career making and designing hats, and established his first couture house in London in the 1930s. There he developed all the signature design elements that he continued to rework throughout his career, believing that there was a limited number of shapes but infinite permutations on them. In 1940, James moved to New York and opened his atelier at 699 Madison Avenue.

? Although this dress was cumbersome to wear—one client reputedly purchased two opera tickets, one for her and one for the dress—James had a devoted following of US socialites. They were prepared to tolerate the designer's volatile temperament and cavalier attitude for the privilege of wearing his gowns. He was reluctant to part with his final creations and overly discriminating about his clients, refusing commissions, and even leaving some garments incomplete or failing to meet deadlines.

Master of color comparatives, of the cut and fold of exceptional cloths.

VOGUE, JUNE 1948

Gernreich became a household name with the introduction of the monokini in 1964 (see pp. 114–115). Other firsts included chiffon T-shirt dresses, hipster skirts for both men and women, see-through blouses and the thong bathing suit, cut high to expose the buttocks. He often experimented with innovative materials, using cut-outs, vinyl and plastic. In his knitwear, he combined Op art-inspired patterns and vivid colour. He received the Coty American Fashion Critics' Award in 1960, 1963 and 1966, and was inducted into the Coty Hall of Fame in 1967.

Psychedelic-print kaftan, 1967
Pucci

Hand-printed kaftan, 1973
Mary McFadden

**UNISEX KAFTAN
RUDI GERNREICH
1970**

Avant-garde designer Rudi Gernreich (1922–85) was the first to formalize interchangeable clothes for men and women, and these voluminous unisex kaftans were representative of the designer's desire to liberate the body from the confines of structured clothing and to break down the sexual and gender barriers in society. Although Gernreich was renowned for his use of partial nudity, worn by the young and slender, when asked by *Life* magazine to preview trends for the forthcoming decade, the designer propounded a theory not only with regard to the equality of men and women and the clothes they wear, but also concerning the different stages of life. His kaftans were designed specifically with the elderly in mind. Created for Expo 1970, held in Osaka, Japan, the printed silk kaftans were inspired by the abstract images of artist Piet Mondrian, with circles, squares and stripes in vivid red, green and blue on black and white. Scattered among the formal geometric design are fragments of text in varying font sizes. The all-enveloping robe was cut to disguise the silhouette, with wide trumpet sleeves and a deep cowl neckline. To complete the unisex look, Gernreich recommended that both men and women shave their heads so that their gender was less obvious.

If a body can no longer be accentuated, it should be abstracted.

California-based designer Gernreich began experimenting with knitted fabrics when he went into partnership with William Bass. He left Bass in 1959 to launch his own label in Los Angeles. In the early 1960s, the designer opened a showroom in New York, where he presented his designs for knitted jersey tube dresses and later sportswear.

Outside high fashion, the sexes were already dressing in a similar style by 1970, with males and females both sporting flowing hair, jeans and variations of the kaftan. The last was worn by the hippy subculture in imitation of the flowing robes of the East, often with shisha embroidery and in light, sheer fabrics. The Gernreich version is more substantial, but was reputedly unappealing to those for whom it was intended.

The lit silhouette of a pin-headed David Byrne is a menacing preamble to a stage performance that continues to have resonance. This is, in part, because *Stop Making Sense* was filmed by director Jonathan Demme over three evenings of live performances at the Pantages Theater in Los Angeles, thereby disseminating the image of the 'big suit' to a much wider international audience.

BIG SUIT FOR DAVID BYRNE
1984

In one of the most iconic images of the 1980s music scene, David Byrne, frontman and founding member of new wave band Talking Heads, wears the infamous 'big suit' for his performance of 'Girlfriend is Better' during the recording of the live concert movie *Stop Making Sense* (1984). With a stage stripped of all extraneous detail—most props were painted in matt black to avoid reflecting light and there was an embargo on coloured lights to illuminate the performers—Byrne appears as an animated rectangular figure, who dances like a marionette (the head and limbs jiggle but the body remains inert). The big suit is cut along traditional lines, with a three-button fastening and narrow revers, but the oversized webbed shoulder pads and a webbed girdle around the waist beneath the pale grey fabric not only create width but also hold the suit away from the body. Viewed from the side, however, the suit presents a normal-sized silhouette. In a scene from the film, Byrne interviews himself and gives tongue-in-cheek reasons for wearing the suit: 'I like symmetry and geometric shapes. I wanted to make my head appear smaller and the easiest way to do that was to make my body bigger, because music is very physical and the body understands that before the head.'

A visit by Byrne to Japan, where he experienced Noh theatre—a form of classical Japanese musical drama, dating from the 14th century, that is structured around song and dance in which movement is slow and stylized and the costumes heavy and cumbersome—influenced the singer in his design of the big suit. The garment also recognizes *Filzanzug* (*Felt Suit*, 1970) by Joseph Beuys; the unyielding outsize felt suit was first worn by the German avant-garde Fluxus artist in *Action the Dead Mouse/Isolation Unit* (1970) and later produced in 'multiples'.

Oversized checked coat, 2012
Thom Browne

Oversized black blazer, 2013
Haus of Gaga

A definitive music genre of the 1980s, new wave was a post-punk movement in which artists differentiated themselves from the showy excesses of contemporary stage acts such as Duran Duran and Culture Club, which had a dressing-up approach to stage costume. By wearing his big suit, Byrne promulgated a more cerebral approach, integral to the performance.

. . . I got on stage and started screaming and squealing and twitching about. Ha! Like, that sure made sense!

DAVID BYRNE

The first Comme des Garçons collection to be shown in Paris in 1981 revolutionized attitudes to fashion and was received with international acclaim. The designer's indifference to the preoccupations of marketability resulted in the infamous 'Hiroshima chic', dubbed the 'bag-lady look' by US journalists owing to its lack of 'hanger appeal'. Kawakubo's introduction of conceptualism included asymmetry, deconstruction and a delight in irregularity and imperfection, which resulted in laddered sweaters and crooked and exposed seams.

Padded asymmetrical top A/W 2010/11
Rick Owens

Knitted top, A/W 2013/14
Sandra Backlund

> It is true to say that I 'design' the company, not just clothes.
>
> REI KAWAKUBO

LUMPS AND BUMPS DRESS
COMME DES GARÇONS
1997

In a collection for her label Comme des Garçons, Japanese designer Rei Kawakubo (1942–) creates a range of unorthodox silhouettes by introducing areas of padding in goose-down feathers that reshape the body. The laws of gravity are reassessed continually throughout the collection, as arbitrary parts of the body are distorted into unfathomable 'lumps and bumps'. Design features include an asymmetrical shoulder, a plumped-up hip, a hump at the top of the back, and, as here, one arm bound tightly to the body in a swathe of blood-red fabric—all of which announce a radical departure from the accepted wearability of mainstream fashion. As if seen through a fairground's distorting mirror, the garments stretch the body in different directions. This effect is emphasized by the use of outsize check gingham, a jaunty homely material in pastel shades that adds further interest to the unconventional forms. The collection led to a collaboration, prompted by *Fashion Projects* (a publication that aims to create a platform to highlight the importance of experimental fashion), between Kawakubo and Merce Cunningham, choreographer of avant-garde ballet. The dance, titled *Scenario*, premiered in 1997 at the Brooklyn Academy of Music in New York.

A fine art and literature graduate of Keio University in Tokyo in 1967, Kawakubo formally established her Comme des Garçons company in 1973, having first adopted the name in 1969. The company's first menswear line was launched in 1978. Kawakubo oversees every aspect of the company's output and the label is now a cohesive independent global brand.

? Worn by the fashion cognoscenti, the monochrome palette and distressed fabrics were universally adopted by the art and media world during the 1980s and 1990s. Today, the designer's influence is now equally revered but less visibly at the forefront of high fashion. Kawakubo is joined in her rejection of fashion orthodoxy by other cult designers, such as Yohji Yamamoto, and London-based label Boudicca.

Certain principles are common to both fashion and architecture—the designed object has to fulfil criteria of functionality and desirability—and both are concerned with 'shelter', although with fashion it is of a more intimate kind. Textiles are infinitely adaptable and can be pleated and folded, reinforced and bonded, to produce an architectonic form, particularly with the aid of techniques such as laser cutting.

ARCHITECTURAL SKIRT
BOUDICCA
2006

Radical design label Boudicca offers a gothic version of the Gibson Girl, an American archetype popularized by illustrator Charles Dana Gibson at the beginning of the 20th century, alongside city-slick tailoring with a twist. High-collared shirts, corseted waists and A-line skirts, as well as jackets and dresses featuring slight leg-of-mutton sleeves, are shown alongside complex deconstructions of the tuxedo. These combine elements of black and white: crisp white wide lapels on a cropped tuxedo jacket, worn with a white asymmetric shirt and a tight buttoned waistcoat tied with an outsize obi bow at the back. Combining the two themes, a white waistcoat worn over all black features a frilled bustle at the back. Here, stark starched white is used for a triangular skirt, created by the designer's experimentation with pleating. It falls from a high-waisted yoke, banded with a length of black leather. Supported by layers of frilled black polyester net, the handkerchief-point hem dips to the knee at the front with volume extending outwards at the sides. The neat cotton shirt, with fine pleating each side of the centre front, partners the skirt and features an Edwardian high-necked collar on a stand, decorated with a brooch. Black rayon stretch knit trousers are worn beneath the skirt.

Avant-garde label Boudicca has an experimental approach to design, one that is more in keeping with Japanese designers, such as Yohji Yamamoto, than its UK-based contemporaries, particularly in its preferred palette of black and white with only intermittent shots of colour. Deconstructing tailoring to redefine the separate components of jackets, suits and dresses, Boudicca combines expert craftsmanship with attention to detail, filling the space between haute couture and ready-to-wear with high-end production values.

Yellow evening dress,
Pre-fall 2013
Roksanda Ilincic

White trouser suit,
A/W 2013/14
Gianfranco Ferré

 Boudicca was founded in 1997 by Zowie Broach (1966–) and Brian Kirkby (1974–). The label showed in galleries across Europe before being invited on to the London Fashion Week schedule in 2001. In 2008, it launched a scent called Wode, after the cobalt-blue woad worn as warpaint by Boudicca, the ancient British warrior queen for whom the label is named.

 [Our goal is] to forge the identity of a future of design that is not just about making clothes, but the craftsmanship.
ZOWIE BROACH

Ghesquière's success as creative director of Balenciaga can be attributed in part to his references to the house's archives. However, the designer also brought a ruthlessly contemporary edge to the label, utilizing the DNA of the brand to pursue his own singular vision. Always at the forefront of current trends, he launched the 'Lariat', a motorcycle-inspired riveted and tasselled handbag, at the height of the obsession with the 'It' bag. His commercially adept eye also resulted in the skinny trouser, which became a fashion staple.

Voluminous dress, S/S 2013
Victoria Beckham

Oversized top, A/W 2013/14
Stella McCartney

EXAGGERATED BELL-SHAPE CAPE
BALENCIAGA
2006

With all the hallmarks—moulded shoulders, complex tailoring, sculptural lines—of the quintessential couturier Cristóbal Balenciaga at the height of his influence, the short caped coat in lustrous brocade was designed by Nicolas Ghesquière (1971–), after researching the company's archives. He introduces new proportions in a collection of cocoon-shaped jackets with stand-away collars, partnered with cropped skirts with folded, unpressed pleats, and peplum jackets in silk gazar, thereby reimagining the couturier's signature lines with verve and a contemporary aesthetic. Balenciaga was the master of the set-in sleeve, which provided a smooth line without bulky creases yet also allowed freedom of movement. Ghesquière replicates Balenciaga's skill in the artful construction of the caped shoulders, which also incorporate the sleeves. These are bracelet-length, another of Balenciaga's signature details, and finish to coincide exactly with the gathers of the deeply frilled dropped waist of the coat. Four fabric-covered buttons feature on the double-breasted front, which is otherwise completely unadorned, with no trace of seams or darts. The neckline is cut away slightly from the base of the neck, adding to the purity of the line.

I think the most beautiful thing for me is to revive this brand and to make sure one of the most incredible names in fashion is alive.

NICOLAS GHESQUIÈRE

Plucked from relative obscurity, French designer Ghesquière was appointed the creative director of Balenciaga in 1997. Previously one of the most revered fashion houses, it had lain dormant since the death of its founder in 1972. Ghesquière successfully repositioned the house and remained head of the label for fifteen years. Citing artistic differences, the designer relinquished his post in 2012.

? Fashion is cyclical. Shifts in emphasis of the silhouette veer over time from body con to architectonic sculptural shapes that stand away from the body. Balenciaga redefined the female silhouette with the introduction of the chemise, or sack dress, in the mid 20th century, when the hourglass figure was prevalent. By revisiting the cocoon-shaped silhouette, Ghesquière set in motion a return to volume.

? The styled-up drama of the image belies the practicality of the garment, the construction of which provides a lightweight all-over protective warmth. The origins of the puffa coat lie in the 1930s, when outdoorsman Eddie Bauer created a prototype jacket with quilted down insulation, which he dubbed the 'Skyliner'. Pioneering active sportswear designer Norma Kamali elevated the puffa jacket to high-fashion status with her mid 1970s fabled sleeping-bag coat, reportedly created while camping in the woods. Since then, variations of the seminal Kamali design have inspired generations of quilted puffa coats.

"

Western clothes are our everyday wardrobe. But I don't think that it makes much of a difference anymore whether you're Japanese or American or European.

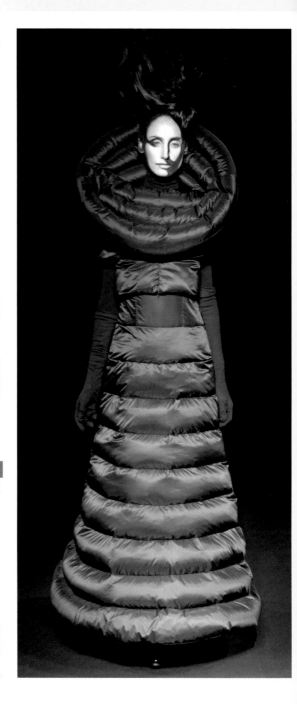

PUFFA DRESS
JUNYA WATANABE FOR COMME DES GARÇONS
2009

With his customary approach of appropriating the mundane and elevating it into far from predictable garments, Japanese-born Junya Watanabe (1961–) transforms a utilitarian puffa coat into a dramatic soft sculpture redolent in silhouette of a 19th-century crinoline. The horizontal circular tubing that makes up the body of the garment in black ciré nylon is interrupted at the waist by a flatter panel before forming a bodice that is divided by a vertical seam for shaping. The deep ruff at the neck is created by more inflated tubing, which frames the head at the back but is concertinaed at the front to allow movement and visibility. The reflective nature of the fabric and the light that gathers at each indented segment transform the inherent heaviness of the dress into something more light and airy. In contrast, fine matt black knitted jersey is used for a skintight turtle-neck top, which reaches the chin and covers the arms, which are also clothed in opaque black gloves ruched to above the elbow. Inherent to the styling of the image is the dramatic maquillage, with the face shaded in black on white to create a visage that appears to have been photographed in deep shadow. Lavish swathes of raven-black hair are coiled over and above the head to reach an asymmetric point.

Based in Tokyo, Watanabe continues to work under the overall Comme des Garçons title, which administrates and produces his collections. Since the launch of his menswear line in 2001, Watanabe has collaborated with established brands such as Brooks Brothers, Levi's, and Lacoste, giving a fresh approach to fashion staples such as the seersucker jacket and denim jeans. His collections are sold from London's Dover Street Market, which stocks brands personally selected by Rei Kawakubo.

Sleeveless puffa jacket, 2013
Isabel Marant

Skirted puffa jacket, 2013
Marios Schwab

High-shine puffa jacket, 2013
Moncler Armoise

A unifying feature of Watanabe's diverse body of work is a respect for the traditional quality of the materials he uses, such as tweed, denim and technically advanced textiles, combined with his unrivalled tailoring skills. Provocation and overt sexuality are notably absent from his runway shows, which are presented in silence.

Watanabe has encouraged his protégé, Tao Kurihara, to launch her own line under the Comme des Garçons label. She presented her first collection in Paris in 2005 to much acclaim.

British-born designer Goldin graduated from Central Saint Martins College of Arts and Design in 2005, and showed her first collections as part of the Fashion East collective. She made her first solo appearance at London Fashion Week in 2008. In 2010, the designer was awarded the Fashion Forward prize from the British Fashion Council for brand investment. After a two-year hiatus from the fashion spotlight, she moved her operations to New York City to show her 2013 collection.

White cut-out dress,
S/S 2012
David Koma

Broderie anglaise dress,
S/S 2012
Vera Wang

ORIGAMI DRESS
LOUISE GOLDIN
2009

Louise Goldin (1978–) boldly engineers complex structures and fabrication to architectural effect by exploiting the properties of fine- and heavy-gauge knitted fabrics. She fashions her futuristic, multilayered pieces using a variety of techniques, such as draping, pleating and folding. The simplicity of sleeveless shifts and see-through mesh dresses vies with intricate origami-like arrangements of cloth and sporty all-in-ones with a faint indication of print, inspired by satellite traces on the Earth's surface. Here, the scalloped three-dimensional bra segments extend into lift-away shoulders, clearing the line of the body and with a hint of American footballer. They are layered over a transparent sporty racer-back vest with an opaque front bib, beneath which is secured a deep frill caught midway beneath the bodice. Mixing visual metaphors, a gladiatorial fold in ice-blue and white stiffened fabric provides an apron-like skirt to mid-thigh at centre front, over a shorter flared skirt beneath. This is attached to a broad yoke that allows a hint of midriff to be displayed. The interplay of transparent and solid fabrics extends to the sheer white shorts, cropped to just below the knee, which fall into natural creases creating a stripe effect. Neat socks and all-white platform shoes are further sporty additions.

In 2009, Goldin designed a forty-piece capsule range in collaboration with Scottish cashmere brand and knitwear manufacturers Ballantyne. It was the first of two collections.

A force behind knitwear innovation, Goldin honed her experimental approach after months spent working in knitwear factories, consulting with expert protagonists of technical development for her collections. However, the craft process never overrides the end product: the collections are fashion first and foremost, and only incidentally knitwear.

? Goldin's ingenuity in fabrication has set the paradigm for the possibilities inherent in contemporary knitwear design. It is axiomatic that the engineering of a contour garment such as a bra will demand the greatest precision of any genre of apparel. It is also evident that the flexible loop structures of warp and weft knitting—from sheer jersey to more robust structures—are the most adept and versatile for this type of clothing. These jersey structures are exploited by designers to generate body-enhancing contours of three-dimensional integrity.

"

I think I've always had an element of sports aesthetic, whether it's in evening wear or daywear and I just sort of evolved from there.

?

Offering an exhilarating new attitude to menswear, Van Beirendonck eschews the finely nuanced changes in men's dress, which rely solely on the width of a lapel or the slant of a pocket for a fashion statement. However, his ebullient and energetic appropriation of eclectic sources does not obscure his mastery of cut and material. The designer continues to inspire a generation of newcomers, including US-born Jeremy Scott and Danish fashion designer Henrik Vibskov of the New Nordic Movement, a 21st-century group of designers from Northern European countries who practise in a variety of media.

"

[In each collection] the ethnic inspiration, different types of tribes and rituals, is always there, as is changing the boundaries of men's fashion and gender: I like tension, and I try to provoke tension.

INFLATED TORSO JACKET
WALTER VAN BEIRENDONCK
2009

Belgian fashion designer Walter Van Beirendonck (1957–) extols the physicality of the male body with a postmodern mash-up of high-end couture textiles and fluorescent PVC. Well-versed in the dialectic of graphic subversion, Van Beirendonck exploits the masculine frame as the canvas for a comic-book manifesto of bearded bacchanalian sexuality. The 'eXplicit' collection of spring/summer 2009 is expressed in outré colour, texture and superhero graphics. A voluminous oversized pneumatic top, resurrected from the 'W&LT' collection of 1996, dominates the silhouette, and the turbo-charged figure is offset by the absurdity of the laser-cut, emerald-green faux beard and foliage, below a resolutely placed bowler hat. The primary-toned plastic of the cropped jacket is an evocation of an inflatable life jacket, but with a six-pack and pecs sculpted either side of the centre-front zip. Valves are placed at strategic points on the body, including at the nipples, biceps and shoulders, punctuating the broad-shouldered silhouette with tiny points. With a provenance in aerodynamic, skintight cycling pants, the heavy-duty Lycra is imprinted with curved lightning flashes of gold on red, which matches the model's nail varnish, accentuating the musculature of the lower body.

In 1983, Van Beirendonck showed his first collection, as part of the Antwerp Six. Working under the label 'W&LT' (Wild & Lethal Trash, or Walt) from 1993 to 1999, he developed a humorous and iconoclastic approach to men's fashion, which was in direct opposition to the sombre-hued and conceptual creations of the Japanese designers then showing in Paris, and the inherent glamour of couture. Van Beirendonck offers a unique combination of high-end production values and elements of popular culture.

Lys Noir evening dress, 1957
Christian Dior

Scarlet corset dress, 1992
Dolce & Gabbana

One-shouldered red satin dress, 2011
Vera Wang

Van Beirendonck has long established a receptive audience for his experimentation with the conventions of clothing, politics, sexuality, art and subcultures. The arbitrary nature of his output is admired for its reckless autonomy and sense of humour. Frequently, he blurs the boundaries between fashion and art, and has collaborated with Austrian artist Erwin Wurm.

Van Beirendonck is director of the fashion department at the Royal Academy of Fine Arts, Antwerp, where he has mentored designers including Raf Simons and Kris Van Assche.

? Theatrical garments function as a marketing tool, and every collection features an unwearable piece that exemplifies an ideal yet also makes a spectacular publicity photograph. Enjoying a reputation for showmanship rather than engaging with fashion feasibility, Viktor & Rolf provides a paradigm of elegance, an image that is articulated fleetingly by the model on the runway, and only to be admired from afar.

**TOPIARY DRESS
VIKTOR & ROLF
2010**

Viktor Horsting (1969–) and Rolf Snoeren (1969–) chop through layers of densely packed silk tulle with the surgical precision of topiarists to create a sculpted three-dimensional exercise in surreal geometry for their eponymous label Viktor & Rolf. The same transparent ice-blue tulle is draped asymmetrically across the front of the strapless, form-fitting, black sheath. The bodice is emblazoned with a deep 'V' plastron of white sequins before erupting into a multilayered tutu shaved into a straight line and cropped at the hips. In a mystifying construction, the lower part of the wide skirt extends outwards and parallel to the interrupted upper component in gravity-defying layers, exposing only a narrow glimpse of the sheathed body at the core. The ponderous weight and volume of the skirt tilt and sway like a 17th-century farthingale. A cloud of pale golden silk tulle billows around the head and is anchored under the chin, echoing the advertisements of the Flowerbomb fragrance launch of 2005. Often referred to as the Gilbert & George of the fashion world, owing to their suited, bespectacled appearance and preference for art installations rather than the runway, Horsting and Snoeren combine technical virtuosity with showmanship.

Positioned at the interface of art and fashion, the design duo began making clothes in 1993 after graduating from the atelier of the Netherlands' prestigious Arnhem Academy of Art and Design. Alongside Maison Martin Margiela and the Antwerp Six, Viktor & Rolf offered a headline-grabbing alternative to the minimalist aesthetic and branding of the 1990s, with the emphasis on high-concept runway presentations.

Butterfly ball gown, 1955
Charles James

Human Bouquet, 1997
Moschino

VOSS dress, 2001
Alexander McQueen

Creation ensemble, 2005
John Galliano

Viktor & Rolf enjoyed a reputation for anarchy and resolute defiance of commercial orthodoxy after its first underground 'couture' show in Paris in 1998. Latterly, Horsting and Snoeren have edited their collections with more direct wardrobe appeal, moving towards the mainstream by launching a ready-to-wear line in 2000 and a successful diffusion collaboration with high-street retailers H&M in 2006.

Astutely manipulating the fashion system for its autumn/winter 1996 collection, Viktor & Rolf produced no clothes at all, instead sending out press releases that read 'Viktor & Rolf on strike'.

Martin Margiela (1957–) launched his first menswear collection in 1998, known as 'line 10'. Each subsequent product range was numbered from 0 to 23, which acted as a reference code rather than as a chronological record. Margiela's refusal to supply a brand name added to his mystique: the white label attached to the outside of the garment with stitches at each corner carried no brand identification or sizing information, but merely served to reassure the cognoscenti of their exclusivity.

BARREL SKIRT
MAISON MARTIN
MARGIELA
2010

The artful suspension of the skirt, seemingly held away from the natural waist with invisible padding, describes an unfamiliar silhouette, and one contrary to the conventional ideal of feminine pulchritude and the hourglass figure. Cut from menswear suiting, the overlong skirt in pearl grey falls to the ground in soft folds, creating a concertina of fabric at the hem. The only interruption in the perpendicular surface is an unexpected narrow red velvet belt, threaded through loops at the topmost edge of the skirt. The smooth surface of the fine-knit turtle-neck sweater in matching pearl grey is produced by the Wholegarment™ method, which utilizes a single thread in one continuous piece and thus removes the necessity for all underarm and side seams. The technology provides a unique aesthetic characteristic, one that is used commonly in performance sportswear, and is in direct contrast to the early days of the label when Maison Martin Margiela regularly exposed the construction of the garment, revealing the seams in a process of reversal. The lightly padded shoulder area and the loosely fitting funnel neckline add to the play on proportions and deliberate ease of fit. The sleeves are manufactured to be overlong, pushed up to create ruched bands of fabric at the wrists.

Padded skirt, A/W 2006/07
Balenciaga

Oversized trousers, 2011
Phoebe Philo for Céline

The Chambre Syndicale de la Haute Couture invited the label to show its first haute couture collection on the official Paris schedule in 2006, an acknowledgement of its expert craftsmanship.

Margiela's work as a deconstructivist not only questions the construction of conventional garments, but also examines the system in which they are produced. Since its inception in 1988, Maison Martin Margiela has been reclaiming pieces under the Artisanal Initiative; each garment is reworked entirely by hand in the atelier in Paris.

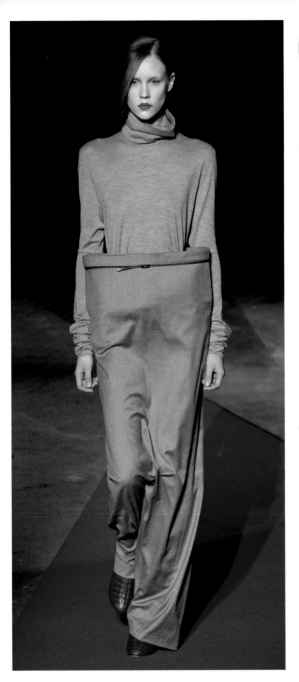

? After Margiela left the Maison Martin Margiela team in 2009, the remaining seventy-one members that make up the collective continued the aesthetic of the label: one that questions established fashion assumptions. The clothes exist independently of any marketing initiative, and garments are presented within an industrial framework rather than in a theatrical display. A more conventional version of the extreme silhouette seen on the catwalk would be offered in the showroom. Here, the skirt would be rendered wearable by the removal of the padding at the waist.

"

As a fashion house we feel it necessary, humanly and creatively, to listen, watch, smell and touch other visions and interpretations, to inspire us and help us define our own.

? A hooped device used to extend the width of a skirt, known as a farthingale, was first introduced in the 16th century. It reappeared in the mid 19th century as the Victorian crinoline. Although the crinoline is now usually confined to bridal and occasion wear, avant-garde designers continue to play with its proportions and structure, as seen in Vivienne Westwood's mini-crini collections of 1985 and 1987.

**BRIDAL GOWN
COMME DES GARÇONS
2012**

An accusation that is frequently levelled at the wide-skirted wedding gown is that it 'looks like a meringue'. Here, Rei Kawakubo (1942–), for her label Comme des Garçons, sculpts the meringue into dollops of asymmetrical padding, some of which have slipped down the face in a perverse sort of wedding veil. The 'White Drama' collection celebrates all the common rites of passage, from the christening and communion ceremonies of childhood to the weddings and funerals that follow. These are shown in variations of lace, tulle and duchesse satin, with cake-like decorations of white-on-white flower petals and sculpted roses. The cage crinoline is the inspiration for most of the bridal wear, but it is constructed outside the garment as a form of exoskeleton rather than in its traditional role of supporting the weight of the dress. Here, the banded hooped crinoline is set beneath the padding of the hips, which comprises solid amorphous shapes of varying sizes that overlap to make a panniered silhouette. The crinoline's infrastructure is left exposed to show the body beneath. A short cape of laser-cut lace, gathered on one shoulder, has a loose grown-on collar and shrouds the upper part of the body, restricting the movement of the arms. Plain white rubber flat-heeled mid-calf boots worn over bare legs add a scientific note of clinical simplicity.

Kawakubo has worked across many disciplines; she introduced her first furniture line in 1983 and launched a biannual cultural magazine, *Six*, in 1988. She has also collaborated with US artist Cindy Sherman and has exhibited her work in museums and galleries throughout Europe.

Creation ensemble,
A/W 2005/06
John Galliano

Cropped crinoline,
A/W 2008/09
Jean Paul Gaultier

I start every collection with one word.... After I find the word, I then do not develop it in any logical way.

REI KAWAKUBO

Although independent of mainstream fashion, Kawakubo nevertheless captures media attention by embodying a couture level of craft integrated into collections of esoteric subject matter. As the owner of an independent label with her own stores, the designer has the luxury of presenting her ideas undiluted, and she is also able to resist the fast turnover of the fashion calendar, which insists on pre-fall, holiday and resort collections as well as seasonal collections.

? Philo was instrumental in heralding a radical change in fashion: one that eschewed drama, spectacle and fantasy for wearable garments with a cooler, unadorned edge for the modern woman. She made it acceptable to bypass the body by playing with new proportions and volumes, inspiring a rush of imitators. Concentrating on daywear separates, Philo streamlines a sportswear vibe alongside perfect tailoring. Together with Clare Waight Keller at Chloé and Stella McCartney, the designer presents a ready-to-wear urban modernity of wearable creativity that is quietly assertive and subtly sexy.

"

I think that to offer women something that feels more about investing in something and less about being disposable is a complete corrective to the world we're in.

PHOEBE PHILO

OVERSIZED COAT
CÉLINE
2012

London-based designer Phoebe Philo (1973–) provided the benchmark for luxurious minimalism with this jumbo-sized coat for French house Céline, redirecting fashion away from souped-up sexually charged clothes to create a new interest in volume. The coat is cut with controlled fullness to cocoon the body loosely, the centre front forming an unbroken line from a single, hidden fastening set just above the waist. Expertly tailored, the sleeves have two seams to provide the necessary fullness and forward curve. The underarm sleeve seam exactly matches the seam that runs from shoulder to hem, broken only by the flap of the slightly slanted horizontal pockets, exactly scaled to match the proportions of the coat. The mainly monochrome collection was shot with details of bright colour, including this colour-blocked cobalt-blue coat. The slouchy envelope bag in conker-colour leather, folded over and tucked under the arm, led the way not only in design, but also by offering a new way of carrying the 'It' bag, thereby signalling the end of the heavy-metalled shoulder bag or lady-like arm candy. The coat is worn over trousers with a track-pant stripe, cropped to just above the ankle to show 1960s-inspired zip-fronted white ankle boots with a square toe.

Philo initially worked as Stella McCartney's design assistant at French label Chloé before succeeding her as creative director in 2001. There, Philo reintroduced the label's signature look of 1970s-inspired high-waisted jeans, vintage-style blouses and filmy dresses sharpened up with military-style jackets. In 2009, Philo was appointed creative director of French house Céline, which was founded in 1945 and is now owned by LVMH. Philo was awarded British Designer of the Year in 2004 and 2010.

Camel cocoon coat,
A/W 2006/07
Balenciaga

Pink plaid coat, A/W 2013/14
Stella McCartney

As creative director of Céline, Philo showed her first collection for the label in autumn/winter 2010/11 and spearheaded a new approach to the house: one of pared-down chic and with a distinct minimalist signature. Deploying colour blocking, disciplined tailoring and luxurious fabrics, Philo implemented a strong silhouette with austere architectural pieces.

During her time at Chloé, Philo produced one of the most coveted 'It' bags of the 21st century. The multipadlocked 'Paddington' bag was introduced in 2005 and rapidly sold out.

Although the Marc Jacobs main line, which was underpinned by LVMH, is informed by the same high-end production values and intensity of embellishment that is seen in the designer's work for Louis Vuitton, in his diffusion line—Marc by Marc Jacobs, launched in 2001—Jacobs combines retro influences with an emphasis on buttons and belts, idiosyncratic prints and sweet details such as the Peter Pan collar. Quirky and playful, the Marc Jacobs aesthetic is finely honed for the more edgy 'It girl', such as long-time friend Sofia Coppola.

Fur-collared coat and hat,
1976
Yves Saint Laurent

Brocade coat, A/W 2012/13
Prada

OVERSIZED HAT
MARC JACOBS
2012

An oversized hat with a face-concealing brim in ruby-red fur and an abbreviated purple cape in felted wool epitomize the luxurious glamour of a collection influenced by the fashions of the golden age before World War I. Visionary designer Marc Jacobs (1963–) heralds the luxury of the era with a collection that is rich in texture and embellishment and that features a palette of forest green, mauve, lilac, grey, black and gold. These are fashioned into skirts, dresses and jackets that re-create a silhouette that bears little relation to the body beneath: the hobble-skirt and high-waisted silhouette introduced by Paul Poiret, hinted at in the gently ovoid-shaped skirts; the soft, rounded shoulder line of the jackets, featuring outsize buttons; and the distinctive wide-brimmed hats. The play on proportion also includes knee-length skirts layered over cropped trousers, worn beneath coats with padded hips. The surface of the fabrics is interrupted by a lavish overlay of holographic appliqués, oversized paisley-rich jacquards and figured brocade, but a hint of restraint comes from the influence of the Pilgrim Fathers. This is seen in the bertha collars on the abbreviated jackets, the square-toed buckled shoes and the simplicity of the knitted and crocheted stoles wrapped around the shoulders and secured with a pin.

Fashion isn't what people need, it's a joy, it's the art of living.

With an irreverent approach epitomized by his infamous grunge collection for classic sportswear label Perry Ellis in 1993, Jacobs consolidated his reputation for street-wise cool. This quality prompted the French conglomerate LVMH to appoint him as creative director to reposition the Louis Vuitton brand, a post that he held until 2013.

Historical revivalism remains a constant theme in fashionable dress, and in this collection, there are impressions of a pre World War I wardrobe. However, without the razzmatazz of the paper castle runway with tumbling stairs and broken pediments, the individual components comprise a contemporary wardrobe of versatile jackets, three-quarter-length coats and empire-line dresses in richly embellished fabrics.

Last seen in the heady days of conspicuous consumption and the all-out excesses of the 1980s, on the hips of flash trash such as Alexis Colby in US cult television series *Dynasty* (1981–89), the peplum has undergone a reappraisal by designers such as Dries Van Noten and Phoebe Philo at Céline for the 21st century. With its origins in the Greek word *peplos* (meaning shawl), a peplum is a flared ruffle that is attached to the waist of a jacket or bodice or to the waistband of a skirt. Contemporary versions are often structured and architectural, as seen in the Koma jacket. The peplum creates the illusion of a hand-span waist, a reason for its continuing popularity.

Renowned for the innovative cut of his body-con dresses, Koma embellishes an architectural and futuristic silhouette with experimental techniques, such as laser cutting. Eschewing prints in the main, the designer has added outerwear to his repertoire and has investigated quilting, stitching and combining textures.

EXTREME PEPLUM DRESS
DAVID KOMA
2012

In a collection that includes references to Louis Icart's Art Deco greyhound paintings and sporty mesh cut-outs on body-con shifts, London-based designer David Koma (1985–) also offers hints of space-age futurism and elements of iconoclast Paco Rabanne in his use of high-tech fabrics and modular-shaped hardware. The 1960s-inspired coordinated dress and jacket feature sequinned interlocking ovals on the skirt of the off-white dress, resonant of Rabanne's chain-mail dresses; the motif is replicated on the centre-front fastening of the box-shaped jacket. This is cropped to the waist with a double hem. The three vertical openings bound in metal show a flash of bright cobalt silk from beneath. Similar horizontal openings, one each side of the waist, have a length of striped silk in cobalt and gold pulled through the opening, creating an outsize peplum and providing the main feature of the outfit. The jacket has perfectly moulded seamless sleeves, forming an uninterrupted line to the neat collarless neckline. The sleeves are cut to display the diagonal stripes of the dress beneath.

Le Bar suit, 1947
Christian Dior

Peplum jacket, 1981
Claude Montana

Pink frilled peplum skirt, 2011
Giambattista Valli

Koma graduated with a distinction in MA Fashion from Central Saint Martins College of Arts and Design, where he won the Best Womenswear Collection of the Year. Awarded the Vauxhall Fashion Scout Merit Award spring/summer 2010, the designer collaborated on a successful line for British high-street store Topshop in 2011. He also received NEWGEN catwalk sponsorship to show at London Fashion Week in February 2012.

With the pink blazer shrunken down to size and the skirt transposed into trousers, they would make perfectly acceptable accompaniments to the collegiate tie, white shirt, cardigan and brogues, and the ensemble would not look out of place on an Ivy League college lawn. In fashion, exaggeration is often used as a ploy to make a point, with the hope that a more refined version of the collection will retain some of the designer's handwriting and intentions. Garments may be reimagined in a less vivid print, or the silhouette minutely adjusted, for them to become wearable options rather than catwalk extremism.

I feel like jeans and a T-shirt have become establishment. Everyone's dressed down. So actually putting on a jacket is the anti-establishment stance.

OUTSIZE BLAZER
THOM BROWNE
2012

In a collection designed by fashion iconoclast Thom Browne (1965–), featuring a shrunken preppy blazer outlined in studs and low-rise trousers revealing a tuft of merkin (pubic wig), the cartoon-like, oversized American football player comes as something of a welcome relief. It is a collection of two halves: one consists of the paraphernalia of S&M punk subculture, including a tartan kilt worn with a matching gimp mask studded with spikes; and the other half features silhouettes that reference the Incredible Hulk with touches of Herman Munster. Here, Browne stretches the sugar-pink blazer across a magnified torso, the shoulder seam of the jacket on a level with the ears. The padded shoulders and arms are reminiscent of a footballer's protective gear, yet the rubber cap and drawn-on goggles infer that swimming is the sport. The narrow mint-green skirt purports to be a single trouser leg, cuffed and pocketed as the original. As ever with Browne, the emphasis is on the layering and the detail: horizontal flapped pockets are bound in white grosgrain ribbon, a cardigan features a vertically striped button-band that matches the strap over the brown brogues, and a green and white tie secures the neck of the crisp collared shirt. The overall look suggests a preppy on steroids.

Browne's interest in fashion was sparked by buying vintage suits and tuxedos and cutting them down to fit while living in Los Angeles. The former business graduate moved to New York in 1997, and embarked on a fashion career by working with a tailor and undergoing design and merchandising experience at a division of Ralph Lauren. Browne's first own-label menswear collection was launched in 2001 and consisted of five suits. Too poor for a runway show, he sold only to friends.

Pink T-shirt and shorts,
S/S 2009
Walter Van Beirendonck

Grey marl ensemble,
S/S 2010
Alexander Wang

Alongside a new generation of menswear designers, including Michael Bastian and Adam Kimmel, Browne offers a uniquely American point of view on contemporary menswear. This is in opposition to the lifestyle merchandise of über brands such as Ralph Lauren, the traditional tailoring of Savile Row and the sexed-up silhouettes of Dolce & Gabbana.

Browne launched a more affordably priced capsule collection called Thom Grey in 2012, and his suits appeared in a Fashion Institute of Technology exhibition of Ivy League style the same year.

CHAPTER FIVE
DISTORTION

The extenuation of the human outline by distortion is one of the most effective ways of creating an image devoid of sexuality, gender, class, culture and age. The bold visual spectacle of David Bowie and his black PVC bodysuit by Japanese designer Kansai Yamamoto, with its mirrored, circular silhouette, makes no reference to the human form. Similarly, avant-garde designers such as Junya Watanabe for Comme des Garçons and Rei Kawakubo consistently misrepresent the natural silhouette to provide a complete transformation in the outlines of the human body.

Yamamoto launched his label in Tokyo in 1971. He built a reputation in both the fashion and art worlds for creating dramatic garments inspired by the traditions of Japanese theatre, putting a sci-fi inflection on kabuki archetypes and using exaggerated silhouettes created by inventive pattern cutting and synthetic textiles. Bowie's first purchase from the designer was the 'woodlands animal' costume for the Rainbow Concert in London in 1972.

STRIPED BODYSUIT
KANSAI YAMAMOTO
1973

Kansai's brave ideas brought Japanese clothes design to the forefront of fashion.

DAVID BOWIE

The glossy black PVC bodysuit from David Bowie's groundbreaking 'Aladdin Sane' tour in 1973 is striking in its exaggerated distortion of the human figure. Referencing the costume tradition of kabuki theatre, the garment constructed by Japanese designer Kansai Yamamoto (1944–) is used to create an alternative silhouette to the waif-like form of the singer, with aggressively curved legs in reflected parabolic contours from waist to feet. Parallel rows of metallic piping start at the breastbone and knee, and extend to the boundaries of the garment, the pattern mirrored either side of the centre front. This bold visual structure adds substance to Bowie's ungendered presence—only one facet of the myriad identities assumed by the musician in his pursuit of self-projection. The singer's hair is cut in a mullet style and dyed a virulent red in contrast to his pallor, which echoes kabuki stage make-up. Bowie was introduced to Yamamoto's work in 1971 when he viewed the designer's first fashion show in London. Having borrowed garments from this collection for his 'Ziggy Stardust' tour (1972), he went on to commission nine outfits for the 'Aladdin Sane' tour the following year. Yamamoto's collection of 1971 bore all the hallmarks of these later commissions, featuring an eclectic mix of Japanese tradition and futuristic textiles.

Oversized suit for David Byrne, from Stop Making Sense, 1984

Backless dress, 2009
Eiko Ishioka

Outfit for Lady Gaga, 2010
Armani Privé

Yamamoto used cultural elements from his own heritage, such as the graphic exuberance of the 16th-century Momoyama period. By subjecting the human form to extraneous geometry, he gave Bowie a stage presence that transcended spectacle and offered visual resonance to his unique sound.

David Bowie provided a unique and galvanizing vision in an artistic and musical world that was suffering a loss of momentum following the energy of the 1960s, and had yet to find a new form of expression. Bowie and his design collaborators challenged the boundaries of what it was to be male or even human, with an appearance that rendered immaterial both age and gender, and provided a conduit for ideas for a generation of young men. Initiating a confluence between high fashion, costume and popular music, his performances had repercussions throughout the art, fashion and music worlds.

? During Miyake's engagement with the fashion industry, which spans four decades, his key concepts set the paradigm for textile innovation and unconventional garment forms, endearing the designer to an informed cultural elite. The museum-quality 'Pleats Please' line was bought for its collectable status, but also provided an off-duty uniform for the avant-garde.

FLYING SAUCER DRESS

ISSEY MIYAKE

1994

The Miyake Design Studio added the flying saucer dress, an architectural exoskeleton of flexible, ridged textile forms, to the 'Pleats Please' line in the 1994 collection. The name makes reference to the flat-pack disc form of the garment, which resembles the collapsed accordion rings of a paper lantern. Inspired by the flexible light artworks of his mentor, US sculptor Isamu Noguchi, Issey Miyake (1938–) began experimenting in the late 1980s with the surface effects of textile treatments, including new methods of pleating that would allow flexibility of movement of the material while also amplifying the gestures of the body. The radially pleated surfaces of glossy polyester in vibrant primary colours form rolling discs that are compressed or extended with movement. This changes the configuration of the bands of colour from narrow to broad, significantly altering the relationship of the coloured panels, which move from rainbow to monochrome and differentiate the neck and shoulders from the remaining tube of colour. The pleating is imposed after the form is cut by enclosing the woven cloth between pre-folded card that radially compresses the polyester into permanent pleats when set with heat and pressure.

Miyake's creative process has consistently explored the relationship between the body and the space in which it resides. The designer developed innovative fabrics that not only incorporated the traditional craft processes of dyeing and weaving and heritage materials but also included the manipulation of new synthetic fibres. As a result, he formed a new school of aesthetics that bypassed conventional notions of the fashionable body.

" I like to work in the spirit of the kimono: between the body and the fabric there exists only an approximate contact.

Miyake was one of three Japanese fashion designers, alongside Rei Kawakubo and Yohji Yamamoto, to eliminate the geographical and aesthetic boundary between the West and the East. The designer founded the Design Studio in Tokyo in 1971, but began to show his collections twice a year in Paris to an international audience. Miyake now restricts his role within the company to research.

Rolling disc dress, 2006
Pierre Cardin

Folded paper dress, 2013
Jule Waibel

Red hooped dress,
A/W 2013/14
Agatha Ruíz de la Prada

Gaultier has progressed from enfant terrible to cause célèbre during a career that has spanned four decades. He worked briefly at Pierre Cardin, Jacques Estérel and the House of Patou, before launching his own design label in 1976 for Mayagor. In 1997, the designer introduced his first couture collection. He received the Council of Fashion Designers of America International Award in 2000 and took responsibility for the creative direction at Hermès in 2003, until his resignation in 2010.

Op art maxi dress, 1960s
Geoffrey Beene

Op art-inspired print dress, 1965
John Bates

Laser-cut Op art dress, 2011
David Koma

Gaultier provided the wardrobe for Madonna's 'Blond Ambition Tour' in 1990. The costumes included conical bra tops and corsets, which pushed the female silhouette to its extreme.

OP ART JUMPSUIT
JEAN PAUL GAULTIER
1996

Superimposing the optical illusions of the 1960s Op art movement on to the contours of a second-skin jumpsuit, quintessential Frenchman and fashion maverick Jean Paul Gaultier (1952–) creates a visual conundrum. The 'cyber suit' is constructed from a nylon and spandex knit, a synthetic elastic fibre invented by DuPont in 1959. It is printed with vertical bands of gold, olive, purple and grey circles, the deeper colours of purple and grey residing towards the centre of the body, where they separate to grant definition to the inner thigh and the front of the hood. The paler gold is sited at the body's extremities; it highlights the breasts and hips, thus creating an effect that is further emphasized by the changing scale of the circles. The streamlined silhouette arises from an unbroken line that runs from the close-fitting hood to the stirrups beneath the feet, adding to the tension of the fabric and revealing an open toe. An exposed zip runs from the crotch to the high collar, which is integral to the hood. At the back of the suit is an appliquéd square panel, featuring a 'cyber' face made up of circles and ellipses, with a halo of gold. Completely enclosing the body, the all-over garment predates the technically advanced sportswear that has been developed, using biomimetics, to minimize drag.

Instrumental in the longevity of the brand is the eclecticism of Gaultier's distinctive repertoire, which draws inspiration from radically divergent cultures, always underpinned by the framework of Parisian chic. Here, the designer explores the concept of futuristic androgynous sportswear; more usually he eroticizes the female body by fetishizing the corset.

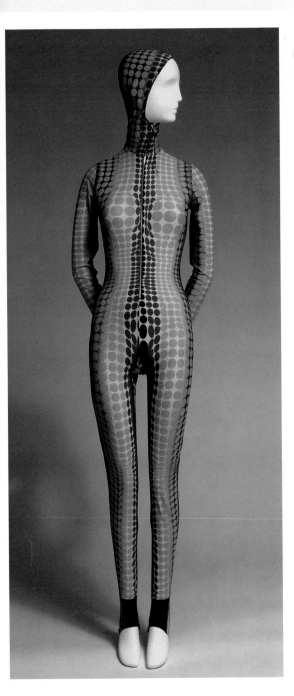

? The distinctive patterning of Op art, usually executed in black and white for greater impact, was adopted by the mass market during the 1960s. British artist Bridget Riley produced her first purely optical work, *Movement in Squares,* in 1961, although the term 'Op art' did not appear until 1964, when *Time* magazine used it to describe optical illusions that utilized bizarre perspectives to fool the eye. Luxe label Louis Vuitton was so allured by the repeating dot patterns of Japanese artist Yayoi Kusama that it commissioned a capsule collection in 2012.

"

Inspiration is never a problem; I usually have too much of it. I sometimes want to say too many things at once.

"

Designers usually buy their material. But for me, it's really important to make the material. Making original material takes a long time.

? The cerebral aesthetic of Hishinuma follows the tradition of Rei Kawakubo and Yohji Yamamoto. These pioneers blazed the trail for the acceptance of Japanese designers on the international fashion agenda when the Chambre Syndicale de la Haute Couture invited them to show as part of the official programme in 1981. While Western fashion is seen in the main to depend upon the re-proportioning of historical styles, Japanese designers break away from fashion codes, rarely defecting from the monochrome. Austere and non-commercial, form is given precedence over content, with a disregard for the conventional notions of beauty and sexuality.

POLYURETHANE DRESS
YOSHIKI HISHINUMA
1999

Yoshiki Hishinuma (1958–) epitomizes the Japanese concept of wabi in this ankle-length dress, constructed of sheer, black polyester and polyurethane. Challenging the Western ideal of fashionable luxury, wabi translates as voluntary poverty, in which imperfection is celebrated, a concept that ironically includes an expensive price tag on hand-crafted clothes. Hishinuma takes this aesthetic further with *wa*, the manifestation that less is more, leaving the black dress unadorned and unrelieved. The designer has replicated the appearance of the fabric being torched by applying polyurethane—a synthetic resin usually used as a varnish for wood—on polyester, resulting in a post-apocalyptic image. The stark all-enveloping shroud has been heat set into chaotically pleated sculptural forms—at one moment evoking the charred residue of traumatized petal shapes, at another forming a fragmented Godzilla-esque silhouette. Although the dress is organic in composition, the distribution of gloss and matt black forms around the body has the graphic discipline of a taschist painting or bamboo brush calligraphy. In addition, there is an echo of the influence of the Gutai group, a Japanese art collective that celebrates the beauty of objects when they become damaged or decayed over the passage of time.

Hishinuma studied at the Bunka Fashion College before working at the Miyake Design Studio in Tokyo. He subsequently became a freelance designer, specializing in costumes for stage productions. In 1992, he began showing his collection in Paris. He was awarded the Mainichi Prize for Fashion in 1996 for incorporating the latest technology into traditional Japanese tie-dye designs. An exhibition of his work was held in 1999 at the Gemeentemuseum Den Haag in the Netherlands.

Mantle, A/W 2001/02
Yohji Yamamoto

Tasselled dress, S/S 2014
Junya Watanabe

Tiered dress, S/S 2014
Comme des Garçons

Hishinuma's clothing concepts have essentially resided in traditional Japanese aesthetics. These span from origami to ikebana, the art of flower arranging. Latterly, the designer has introduced more commercial pieces, returning to show in Paris with an updated look that explores a softly draped geometry, redolent of the opulent curves of exotic blooms.

Hishinuma designed costumes for the ballet *Arcimboldo 2000*, staged by the Nederlands Dans Theater. They were described as 'fantasy confections (tinged with witty period details)'.

Avant-garde designer Watanabe, under the aegis of Rei Kawakubo at Comme des Garçons, is one of the second generation of Japanese designers to follow in the footsteps of the original cohort, Kenzo in 1970, Issey Miyake in 1973 and Yohji Yamamoto in 1981. They created a new language of aesthetics that offered a personal perspective. Welcomed into the French fashion establishment and showing in Paris, these Japanese designers were instrumental in redefining clothing and fashion, as well as promulgating fresh notions of beauty.

Red rubber ruff, 2009
Atsuko Kudo

Black dress with ruff,
A/W 2011/12
Osman Yousefzada

OUTSIZE RUFF
JUNYA WATANABE FOR COMME DES GARÇONS
2000

Radical fashion designer Junya Watanabe (1961–) frequently incorporates complex tailoring into simple lines, to which he adds extraordinary features such as futuristic headpieces or, in this example, an extravagant outsize ruff. The minimal, sleeveless sheath dress from the 'Techno Couture' collection is worn beneath massed organza frills. The dress is constructed from cellophane panne velvet, the two narrow tiers at the hem flipping out slightly at the knee to form an A-line silhouette. With Watanabe's customary injection of asymmetry and his token gesture of deliberate imperfection, the dress is cut and draped to create a slight imbalance in the movement of the side seams, as if it has been inadvertently cut off-centre and pulled to one side. Blending function and delicate beauty, the honeycomb ruff in pale greige organza and silver polyester is separate to the dress. The fullness is tilted towards the front, rather than the back, unlike the original ruff. In a flourish of frills, formed with mathematical precision into a concentric whorl of corolla that decrease in size towards the apex, the face of the model forms the centre of an open flower. Watanabe's inherent practicality ensures that the ruff is a portable accessory, collapsing down into a small looped rectangle that is stored in an envelope.

Sometimes I cannot achieve what I really want to do in just one collection, so in the following collection I do it again.

Utilizing technologically advanced fabrics and techniques allied to his architectural construction and purity of vision, Watanabe creates clothing for men and women. He relies on a mainly neutral colour scheme of black, white and grey for his sculptural garments, which are generally devoid of Western gender markers without being androgynous in intent.

Watanabe is seduced here by the possibilities inherent in the face-framing ruff, which was first seen in European dress in the 16th century. Ruffs evolved from a small frill, produced by a tasselled drawstring at the neck of the shirt, to become a separate garment, which over time increased in size until it completely encircled the head. Watanabe's version is allowed to fall free, rather than be supported by an 'underpropper'.

McQueen's visual representation of other cultures was generally focused on a single image rather than on a collection of cultural ephemera. The designer reputedly disliked travelling, so his research trips were of the imagination rather than rooted in reality. His romanticism harnessed the power of the imagination to envision the unexpected and to escape the confines of the familiar.

RECONFIGURED KIMONO
ALEXANDER McQUEEN
2001

The 'VOSS' collection by Alexander McQueen (1969–2010) was staged inside a huge two-way mirrored box, in which the audience was reflected in the glass before the show began. It featured disparate juxtapositions and moments of theatre, such as a dress made from razor-shells and an ostrich-feather dress with a bodice composed of glass medical slides painted red. The designer's version of the kimono was a single gesture towards chinoiserie, a style inspired by art and design from China, Japan and other Asian countries in the early 18th century. McQueen often reconfigured the kimono; here, he superimposes on to the garment elements of the straightjacket, in keeping with the asylum theme of the collection. It is cut from a smooth-faced, bird's-eye wool cloth, highly embellished with Chinese pheasants and chrysanthemums embroidered in silk thread. The deep, square sleeves of the kimono are extended to bind the arms tightly to the torso. Devoid of any overt construction details or openings, the knee-length jacket seals the body like a carapace. The large rectangular hat, resonant of a window box, is decorated with a fringe of moss-green catkin-like cymes of densely packed flowers from the Amaranthus plant.

'VOSS' was the first collection under his own name for McQueen after he renounced his position as creative head of the heritage house Givenchy, where he had become familiar with the quality of the fine workmanship undertaken in the French haute couture atelier. The designer brought this understanding to his own label, which, when allied to his tailoring expertise, resulted in a seminal collection.

The centrepiece of the 'VOSS' collection was a macabre tableau inspired by Joel-Peter Witkin's photograph *Sanitarium*, dating from 1983. Four glass walls of a box open slowly; they shatter from the impact as they hit the floor, thus releasing several hundred moths into the air. A masked figure, writer Michelle Olley, reclines supine on a chaise longue and is naked apart from a breathing tube attached to her face.

Chinoiserie dress, 2005
Roberto Cavalli

Origami evening dress,
S/S 2007
John Galliano for Dior

Warrior jacket, S/S 2011
Haider Ackermann

Qianlong vase dress, S/S 2012
Mary Katrantzou

'Alexander McQueen: Savage Beauty', curated by Andrew Bolton at the Metropolitan Museum of Art in New York, was the fourth most attended exhibition worldwide in 2012, with more than 661,000 visitors.

Horsting and Snoeren were spotted at a French talent contest in Hyères in 1993, a year after their graduation from the Netherlands' Arnhem Academy of Art and Design. They produced their first fashion/art installation, 'L'Hiver de l'Amour', at Paris's Musée d'Art Moderne in 1994, and by 1997 Viktor & Rolf was a fully established label, invited to show in Paris. The brand discarded couture in 2000 to concentrate on the launch of a ready-to-wear line, only to make a couture comeback in 2013 following an indifferent reception to its later ready-to-wear collections.

'La Poupée' collection, S/S 1997
Alexander McQueen

'Son of Sonzai Suru' collection, 2010
Hussein Chalayan

SCAFFOLDING DRESS
VIKTOR & ROLF
2007

Rejecting the notion that the clothes are more important than the way in which they are presented, Dutch designers Viktor Horsting (1969–) and Rolf Snoeren (1969–) seemingly suspend their runway models from heavy steel rigs, complete with tungsten lights and speakers, as if they are on a giant conveyer belt. In contrast to the technology on display, conventional design components of a folkloric-inspired blouse are evident in the garment, including an all-over print of minute diamonds and spots worked into full-length, tight-fitting sleeves, gathered into puffs above the elbow. A narrow, pointed Peter Pan collar is piped in checked braid to match the cuffs, and small areas of red-and-blue check smocking feature each side of the centre-front fly fastening. All the components are stretched and distorted into a travesty of a garment that shields the viewer from the complex structure that holds the lights aloft and that is shouldered by the model. Similarly, the hem of the skirt is caught up, creating a large circle of sewn-down pleats that come together at the waist and end at the knee. More folksy details are seen in the cobalt-blue embroidery on the black jacquard woven braid, pinned into a rosette at the waist. The Netherlands' decorative heritage is also evident in the embellished clunky high-heeled wooden clogs.

[Fashion] is an aura, an escape from reality. . .a glossy fairy-tale world made real.

With support from the Dutch government and the Groninger Museum, Horsting and Snoeren were able to indulge their avant-garde approach to fashion without the need for commercial viability. In pushing the boundaries of the accepted fashion norm, they inspired a new generation of Dutch designers.

As the leading provocateur of fashion, Viktor & Rolf attracts generous press coverage for its runway installations, thereby gaining the publicity necessary for the success of its ready-to-wear collections. Released from the extraneous scaffolding and re-proportioned from arbitrary distortions in scale, the garments are distilled into a conventional outfit of two pieces: a skirt and blouse.

? The influence of the Japanese aesthetic on contemporary fashion is no longer as potent as it was in the 1980s and 1990s, when designers such as Rei Kawakubo and Yohji Yamamoto were favoured by the fashion elite. However, Watanabe remains the prerogative of those who opt for an innovative cut and manipulation of material rather than for the branded look of a global luxury brand. Unlike many of his Western counterparts, Watanabe refutes the necessity for a themed narrative or for revisiting the past, concerned only with his singular aesthetic of ruthless asceticism.

"

The people who buy my clothes take fashion seriously. They get a kick out of the challenge of wearing something new. Those are the people I design for. I am not interested in the mainstream.

DRAPED DRESS AND HEAD WRAP
JUNYA WATANABE FOR COMME DES GARÇONS
2008

Subverting the classical art of draping and cutting cloth exemplified by Madame Grès and Madeleine Vionnet in the 1920s and 1930s, Junya Watanabe (1961–) manipulates geometric forms such as squares and circles into a contemporary version of Grecian-inspired draping. Although the choice of cloth and colour is austere, a charcoal-grey jersey, the folds at the hip are redolent of the panniered *robe volante* of the 18th century. This period also featured outlandish headdresses that reached absurd heights, interpreted here in an edifice constructed from differently sized balls secured within a cloth to form an undulating surface. The same cloth envelops the face, thus creating a distorted outline to the head. A self-bound, wide, shallow neckline is the only formal component in the construction of the dress; the remaining silhouette is a complex arrangement of intricately draped fabric cut to flow in different directions. The sleeves are not differentiated from the body of the garment and fall loosely from the shoulder point to cover the hand. An asymmetrical fold from waist to hip provides an unexpected acknowledgement of the body, interrupting the loose flowing surface of the garment. Bringing the silhouette back to the norm is a narrow mid-calf skirt with a raw-edged hem.

After leaving Tokyo's Bunka Fashion College in 1984, Watanabe began his career as a pattern cutter at Comme des Garçons under the aegis of founder Rei Kawakubo. In 1987, he was promoted to chief designer of the Tricot knitwear line, and in 1992 Kawakubo gave her protégé the opportunity to design his own collection under the Comme des Garçons umbrella. The Junya Watanabe Comme des Garçons label was launched in 1993 and the designer began showing in Paris that same year.

Pyjamas and scarf, 1931
Madeleine Vionnet

Draped evening gown, 1937
Madame Grès

Black draped dress, 1983
Comme des Garçons

Challenging the conventions of proportion that are associated with high fashion, Watanabe offers an aesthetic that combines technically creative pattern cutting with avant-garde deconstruction. Wearable origami, the garments are simple in shape but inherently complex in construction and in the use of unexpected materials.

Japanese-born designer Watanabe collaborated on a men's and women's ready-to-wear range with Spanish luxury label Loewe in 2013; it featured a collection of leather and denim.

? Body armour and fashion are inextricably linked: since its inception, armour has influenced civilian fashion, and vice versa. Used to both protect and identify the wearer, each armoured component—helmet, gorget, breastplate and leg protection—has provided inspiration for fashion designers. These iterations include Thierry Mugler's cyborg suit in 1995 and the delicate armour-inspired dress by Balenciaga in 2003.

KENDO ARMOUR
GARETH PUGH
2008

Gareth Pugh (1981–) creates bleak apocalyptic nuances with his hybridization of Kendo armour and the ridged scales of mutant invertebrate creatures. He extends extraneous, armour-like protuberances from the silhouettes of the collection by utilizing an extensive array of intimidating materials. These include quantities of monkey fur sprouting from shoulders and shaped into pantaloons. Pugh's dark vision encompasses male warriors with pointed Samurai helmets and women with cantilevered shoulder pads and extruding peplums wrought from zippers. The same fasteners are used to construct this dress: laid horizontally, they form the stiffened undulating folds of a skirt that falls to a point at the front. A corset-like band at the waist is created using more zips, leading to a fitted bodice with two parabolic jersey inserts framing the breasts. The grown-on neckline, long, tight sleeves and corrugated, ribbed leggings create further connotations of reptilian scales and articulated insects, the emphasis consolidated by the antennae-like plaits emerging from the forehead of the model. Elsewhere, black leather is quilted into light-reflecting, diagonally cut squares, manipulated into three-dimensional pyramids, used for a catsuit and to provide the rolling hem of a jersey dress.

Pugh's arcane vision and dark fantasy are mediated through the use of futuristic substances, such as inflated PVC, latex, leather and plastic acrylic sheet. He exploits these materials to distort the human body beyond its notional perimeter, extending personal space into the surrounding area. His sculpted armour is resonant of the aggressive version of femininity propounded by designers such as Thierry Mugler and Claude Montana in the 1980s, with an emphasis on wide shoulders and peplumed skirts.

The Overlook,
A/W 1999/2000
Alexander McQueen

Metallic armour dress,
S/S 2007
Dolce & Gabbana

After graduating in 2003, Pugh held an internship with Rick Owens at the furrier Revillon in Paris and met Owen's wife, fashion consultant Michelle Lamy, who became his backer in 2006. In 2008, the Association Nationale pour le Développement des Arts de la Mode (ANDAM) gave Pugh its international award, enabling the designer to show in Paris.

My collections are autobiographical. I don't need to go to the library and look in a book to see the boot I want to make.

With fans including hip-hop artists such as LL Cool J and Dizzee Rascal and high-visibility pop princess Madonna, De Castelbajac is once again the leading exponent of pop fashion. Influenced by the work of Andy Warhol, Jean-Michel Basquiat and Keith Haring, he continues to acknowledge a wide range of genres, although Pop art remains the overarching basis of De Castelbajac's oeuvre. His avant-garde output includes a dress featuring a Campbell's soup can and garments emblazoned with Haring's vibrant imagery.

Teddy-bear coat, 1988
Franco Moschino

Cartoon-print dress, 2006
Jeremy Scott

LEGO® SUIT

JEAN-CHARLES DE CASTELBAJAC

2009

Recalling childhood memories with his customary ebullience, Jean-Charles de Castelbajac (1949–) hijacks the well-loved construction toy LEGO® for a collection of menswear and womenswear titled 'JC in the Sky with Diamonds'. Never one to cut a joke short before exploiting its potential, the designer showcased the collection with an animated film, directed by Fabrice Pathier, featuring LEGO® figures on the catwalk in front of a LEGO® audience, including a bespectacled and bobbed Anna Wintour on the front row. The suit is cut along conventional lines with a slimline one-button jacket, featuring flapped pockets and narrow lapels, worn with straight-legged flat-front trousers. Only the all-over polychromatic print of LEGO® pieces guarantees eye-popping attention. The suit is worn over a conventional white shirt, with a black silk outsize bow tied beneath the collar, and with platform trainers. The same scale matching print is used for a substantial rucksack, providing a distorted silhouette as the model becomes an automated doll driven by a back-held battery. In a nod to the designer's iconic teddy-bear coat from 1989, a LEGO® version of the toy perches on top. The building blocks are also used to construct eyewear.

> *The 1990s saw me go from US Vogue to ghetto fabulous.*

De Castelbajac launched his own label in 1975 and became one of France's new designers of the burgeoning ready-to-wear industry. He was also one of the first to propose the idea of fashionable sportswear in the 1980s. The designer continues to cultivate his own artistic practice of cartoon-inspired paintings and held his first solo art exhibition 'Triumph of the Sign' in 2009.

Known as the 'king of cartoon' at the height of his popularity, De Castelbajac was one of the first designers to incorporate cartoon images into garments, when, in 1978, he created a range of intarsia knit sweaters that featured Felix the Cat, Snoopy and Bugs Bunny. His postmodern witty and irreverent approach continues to influence a number of designers, including Henry Holland and Giles Deacon.

Consistently reaffirming her ethos of deconstruction, Kawakubo continues to set the paradigm for those designers who choose to inhabit the interface between fashion and art, such as London-based designer Hussein Chalayan. Other recognized deconstructionists include Martin Margiela and Xuly Bet; both allow the construction of the garment to be visible on the surface, rather than hidden from view as is the case with traditional couture and mainstream fashion.

**TWINNED GARMENT
COMME DES GARÇONS
2011**

Rei Kawakubo (1942–) of Comme des Garçons reconfigures disparate garment fragments from fashion staples, such as blazers and parkas, and places them in disjointed balance around the body. Coats are slung horizontally over shoulders or tucked upside-down into waistbands, leaving sleeves to trail behind as the clothing travels a further circuit of the human frame; other garments are constructed from two separate jackets—one long, one short—set in confrontation over wide-legged striped trousers or balloon-shaped skirts. However, the sculpted compositions of leather and jersey show little evidence of disguising the mechanics of construction. On one level, the collection explores notions of inversion, counterpoint and chirality, as well as handedness, demanding that human precepts of balance accommodate the dominance of left or right, and inside as opposed to outside. The progression of this topological argument through the collection eventually arrives at its denouement: the doppelganger opposition of mirrored identity is embodied in linked garments enswathing twin models. Just as identical twins have close bonds and are the result of a mirrored split of a single zygote, the two for one (or one for two) garment is a loosely symmetrical confection of mirrored composites: the game of two halves linked by an ethereal web, symbolizing the inseparable connection of twins.

Over many seasons, Kawakubo has sustained the principle of conceiving each collection as a single composition, determined by a core idea that is then elaborated, reiterated and entwined with subordinate themes. Her ideation owes much to deconstructive theory and, over several decades, it has added a level of serene detachment from more ephemeral tendencies of fashion. Kawakubo's key area of address is the dismemberment of symmetry and formal balance, with a view to establishing a new equilibrium, largely independent of precedent, symmetry and logic.

The Overlook,
A/W 1999/2000
Alexander McQueen

Back-to-front shirts, S/S 2009
Maison Martin Margiela

Kawakubo is the progenitor of radical fashion. Her sartorial vision is memorialized in the art gallery and the museum rather than on the shop floor, unless the shop is one of her carefully controlled outlets, such as the London store Dover Street Market.

I think that pieces that are difficult to wear are very interesting.
REI KAWAKUBO

The daughter of a leading architect and a Catalan aristocrat, Ruíz de la Prada expresses all the playful ebullience of her native Spain across a wide range of lifestyle products in addition to clothing. She is one of an increasing number of designers, such as Eley Kishimoto and Orla Kiely, who successfully practise brand cohesion. The prolific designer has fifteen perfumes to her name, made in collaboration with perfumer Puig. In 2011, she was awarded the 'Lorenzo il Magnifico' Lifetime Achievement Award at the Florence Biennale.

Two-dimensional rectangular coat, S/S 2011
Maison Martin Margiela

Pop art poncho, S/S 2012
Tommy Hilfiger

RECTANGLE DRESS
AGATHA RUÍZ
DE LA PRADA
2011

In a collection that features circles, hearts and squares in an explosion of vibrant colour inspired by the Pop art movement, Agatha Ruíz de la Prada y Sentmenat (1960–) affirms her position as one of Spain's most inventive and playful designers. The heart is a recurring motif throughout the collection: padded and appliquéd to the bodice of a dress, described in blue and copper lamé or laser cut into ever-decreasing rows. Elsewhere, the circles and target motifs of Pop art are positioned to form the whole garment, rendered as a circle of red dropped over one shoulder on a livid-green coat, or an outsize acid-yellow spot reaching from waist to hem. The silhouette is also inspired by the 1960s, with simple little shift dresses and edge-to-edge coats. The rectangular dress is the statement piece of the collection; the geometry that is hinted at in other garments is here pushed to the limits of wearability. A rectangular frame is pierced at the sleeve and neck to allow the model to push through her arms and neck. There is a gap in the lower seam for her legs, and the overall effect is not unlike an animated sandwich board. The broad bands of colour, moving from warm to cool, are differentiated with a single narrow white stripe at the top, which matches the white brim of the orange beret.

> *The most natural thing in my life is to mix colours. It is absolutely in my nature. I can do that without getting bored for years and years.*

Leading Spanish designer Ruíz de la Prada made her debut in 1981 in her home town of Madrid, where she is a leading cultural figure. Her extensive design repertoire is shown on an international stage and includes childrenswear, which she has shown at the Pitti Immagine Bimbo in Florence since 2001, menswear, shoes and homeware products.

A showstopper piece serves not only to emphasize the theme of a collection, summing up a particular point of view, but it also affirms the handwriting of its designer, which may then be applied across a wide range of products. Ideas that are deemed impractical on the catwalk may well translate into other areas, such as surface pattern on interior products or childrenswear, all within the designer's remit.

Tisci brings a unique point of view and a particular vision to couture craftsmanship. The two- or three-piece trouser or skirt suit is a fashion staple of tailored daywear and a benchmark of the couturier's art. It has its origins in the 'tailormade' of the late 19th century, and contemporary designers continue to reimagine the components into high fashion, varying only the details, embellishment and cloth.

OVOID JACKET
GIVENCHY
2013

Heralding a return to the refined and elegant vision of Givenchy, at a time when the couture house was at its most influential, creative director Riccardo Tisci (1974–) revisits the streamlined and minimal 1960s. Among a collection that also features the designer's signature darkly gothic use of black organza ruffles and ruched blouses with voluminous bishop sleeves in black silk, the trouser suit in palest pearl grey represents clean, modern tailoring. Ending just below the hips, the jacket is double-breasted and secured with two pairs of buttons. The back and front of the jacket are cut into a parabola, the curve extending beyond the body to create a two-dimensional saucer shape. This is caught just above the elbow to form a cape-like sleeve. Asymmetry is supplied by the positioning of the three pockets, one on either side of the waist and a further one sited over the breast; all are horizontal. Two almost imperceptible darts emerge from the pockets up to the bust point, providing minimal shaping. The same grey fabric is used to form a split tabard, worn over narrow, cigarette-shaped trousers. With a nod to Tisci's gothic aesthetic, a wide choker, matching the metal decoration on each hip, is worn beneath another archetypal 1960s garment: the fine white roll-neck sweater.

Unlike the aristocratic Hubert de Givenchy, Tisci was the son of an Italian greengrocer and relatively unknown in 2005, when he was appointed to head the couture house. His previous experience included working with Antonio Berardi and Ruffo Research before he launched his eponymous label in 2004. In 2008, Tisci took over the menswear and accessories collections, in addition to the womenswear. In 2013, the label announced that it would no longer show couture collections to the press, focusing instead on private clients and celebrity dressing.

Trouser suit in powder grey, 1972
Pierre Cardin

Outsize blazer, S/S 2011
Stella McCartney

The appointment of Tisci as creative head of the heritage house Givenchy in 2005 was met with some incredulity by the conservative establishment of haute couture. His gothic, often melancholic aesthetic was in direct contrast to the cool and diffident chic of earlier clients of the house, such as style icons Audrey Hepburn and Jacqueline Kennedy.

Dynamism and romance. That's what I bring to the brand.
RICCARDO TISCI

Oversized knitted coat,
A/W 2009/10
Giles

Oversized knitted cardigan,
A/W 2013/14
Costello Tagliapietra

**OUTSIZE CARDIGAN
SISTER BY SIBLING
2013**

The whimsical and idiosyncratic approach of the Sister by Sibling label is expressed by subverting classic, traditional knitwear designs and techniques into extraordinary pieces. In a tightly edited collection, styled by the influential Katie Grand and inspired by 1980s vamp Paula Yates, presenter of the cult television show *The Tube* (1982–87), lacy raschel-knitted skirts feature alongside subverted Fair Isle stitch and intarsia florals all in sugar-sweet pastel colours offset by black. Here, although the garment retains the conservative features of the traditional knitted cardigan with sleeves and a centre-front fastening, the Sister by Sibling version is a cocoon-shaped three-dimensional outsize knit in palest turquoise. Worn over a pair of brief black pants only, the hand-knitted cardigan dress is constructed on jumbo-sized needles in macro poodle stitch from roving: loose, untwisted bundles of wool fibres. The scarf features the same gargantuan stitch, while the outsize tam-o'-shanter with matching pom-pom is structured more simply in reverse purl stitch. The sleeves of the cardigan end just above the wrists, which are clothed in black fur muff cuffs. Sporty high-top trainers challenge the prettiness of the garment. The impact of the disproportion of the mega detail conflicting with the size of the garment evokes the ersatz miniature clothing of a Barbie doll.

The Sister by Sibling label was the recipient of NEWGEN sponsorship for womenswear for spring/summer 2014, and Sibling won the European section of the International Woolmark Prize in 2014.

Initially a knitwear brand, Sister by Sibling reworks and subverts classic garments and techniques to playful effect. The label has also introduced new textures, such as crochet, and produces stand-alone pieces in denim. Of the three designers, it is Sid Bryan (1974–) who is the self-confessed textile geek and stitch innovator. Joe Bates (1967–) creates the overall look and Cozette McCreery (1968–) heads the PR department and also deals with sales and production.

Sister by Sibling was launched in 2010 as an offshoot of the men's brand Sibling, founded in 2008. Before setting up Sibling, the designers each worked for various brands and design houses, with Bryan designing knitted catwalk pieces for fashion luminaries such as Alexander McQueen, Lanvin and Giles.

Knitwear as a high-fashion statement fluctuates in popularity from season to season and from decade to decade. Sister by Sibling contributes playful adventures in scale and texture to a versatile genre that includes Scottish heritage knits in cashmere by Christopher Kane, chunky hand knits by Jonathan Saunders and pictorial statement sweaters, not seen since the 1980s, by Riccardo Tisci for Givenchy.

Koshino has secured a niche in the firmament of Japanese design by adhering to her unbridled appetite for kitsch showmanship. Her aspiration for much of her work is not only ambassadorial but also editorial: the aim of the Sambadrome exercise was to represent 'contemporary Japan, the Japan of the future' in an allegorical fantasy.

DRESS OF RIDGED TUBES
JUNKO KOSHINO
2013

The Baroque futurism that Junko Koshino (1939–) projects in her carnival confections for a contest at São Paulo Sambadrome has the same outré theatricality that is displayed in many of her catwalk presentations. Koshino designed the outfits, including the key piece that she chose to sport on her own diminutive frame, in support of contestants from the Faculdade do Samba (a samba school), in the blue-collar Jabaquara district. This association is symbolic of diversity in Brazilian society and includes locals from Jardim Oriental, an area that has a large Japanese community. The metallized lamé jersey constructions, devised and styled by Koshino, are potentially an echo of the cross-fertilized cultures of São Paulo. The designer's playful vision is a concoction that leaps from a silhouette evocative of an acolyte of the Minoan snake goddess to a fleeting recollection of a 1950s robotic space toy, all seemingly underpinned by the application of advanced heating and ventilation principles. The hourglass silhouette is nevertheless adhered to, with the emphasized corseted waist leading to a tubular version of the crinoline that extends in width towards the hem. The bodice is low-cut, revealing the breasts, and Koshino's formidable visage is framed by a bi-coloured monochrome wig.

Koshino is a specialist in costume design for theatre and the music industry, and also designs for sports teams. She was appointed a Yokoso! Japan Ambassador by the Ministry of Land, Infrastructure, Transport and Tourism in 2008.

Underlying Koshino's exuberance is an engagement with Japanese 'hyperculture' that emanates from Japan's culture of technological futurism and the hyperbolic mannerism of ceremonial Noh and kabuki theatre. These influences periodically inflect the styling of all manner of products, including the Rococo Japanese automobiles of the 1970s. They can also be seen in the contemporary street outfits of adolescents that frequent the Harajuku district of Tokyo.

Minaret dress, 1995
Issey Miyake

'Hybrid Holism' collection,
A/W 2012/13
Iris Van Herpen

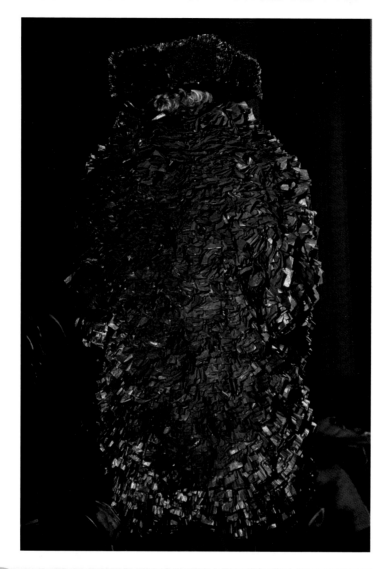

The assignment of cheap disposable plastic to the construction of garments has a heritage that spans four decades. A staple of do-it-yourself nihilism in the peak period of punk, the principle is revisited from time to time, either ironically as in the case of Moschino's ball gown in 1994 or as a genuine homage to punk precedents and to Arte Povera, in which the everyday is elevated to new meaning.

BIN-BAG COAT
GARETH PUGH
2013

Into the iron frosts of the deep-forested wildernesses of Eastern Europe, Gareth Pugh (1981–) lets loose a feral bearskin coat built from ribbons of black plastic. Sculpted with the bulbous excess of an 1980s Valkyrie in monkey furs, the departing hulk signals a subjugation of high culture and formality to the dark forces of the wild. This concludes an autumn/winter collection that sustains an elegiac transition from the pristine orthodoxy of heavily structured liturgical garb to the disintegration of form and fabric as the darkness descends on the runway. At the outset, stark white monolithic cassocks suggest an endless snowscape, free from a horizon but bordered with leafless silhouettes of naked trees, bereft of colour. White gives way to grey, and inevitably black supersedes all other tones as models afford only fleeting views on a transept catwalk, almost as if passing between trees. Changes in material mark the passage from order to disorder: when a few ribbons escape from a complete blanket of woven plastic, they presage the eruption of complete surfaces of layered ends. With a hint of both topiary and Hasidic headwear, Pugh concocts a woven bin-bag finale that confounds the preceding A-line emphasis and recollects the 'destroy' instincts of the core values of punk.

Pugh has risen from playful enfant terrible to a seer who commands respect for his complex vision and sophisticated eye. His ability to create an imaginative trajectory from the wearable to the awe-inspiring hinges on a confidence that is not self-indulgent but has evolved to become both skilful and uncompromising. If the story demands bear-like bin-bag extravagance, Pugh is prepared to make the proposal a reality. The ranges are now seeded with key pieces that are viable in both fashion aptness and Pugh's distinctive design outlook.

Asymmetrical dress,
S/S 2008
Lanvin

Black patchwork skirt,
S/S 2009
Comme des Garçons

Since his debut of riotous irreverence, Pugh has retained his appetite for being daring, but this is now mediated through an elegant theatricality rather than in his initial vein of vaudevillian excess. The designer has developed a sophisticated ability to sustain a progressive narrative in his collections, which rarely deviate from a rigorous monochrome palette.

In the exhibition 'Punk: Chaos to Couture' at the Metropolitan Museum of Art in New York in 2013, five of Pugh's heavily layered bin-bag garments were used to exemplify 'DIY: Bricolage'.

Green studied at Central Saint Martins College of Arts and Design before interning with both Walter Van Beirendonck and Henrik Vibskov. His graduate collection was displayed at the 'ARRRGH! Monstres de Mode' exhibition at La Gaîté Lyrique, Paris, in 2013. The same year he presented his autumn/winter collection at the first London Collections: Men schedule; it was inspired by the designer's fascination with light and dark.

Distressed sweater,
A/W 2011/12
James Long

Zip-front jacket and cropped trousers, S/S 2014
Bobby Abley

Shadow-print suit, S/S 2014
Yohji Yamamoto

Green customized David Beckham's red, white and blue Adidas sneakers for the Olympic Opening Ceremony in 2012. His own-name range of shoes, in collaboration with Purified Footwear, launched in 2014.

SCULPTURED HEADPIECE
CRAIG GREEN
2013

With a form of unfinished, rough-hewn, do-it-yourself Cubism, cast in an austere monastic palette, British designer Craig Green created a press furore with his dramatic, all-concealing facial masks. Reportedly constructed from found fence panels in addition to pieces bought from a do-it-yourself store, the moving sculptures nevertheless accompany a collection of commercially viable pieces. Pitched as an allusion to a theme of shadows and reflections, each black outfit on the runway is a replica of a cream one in front. Here, the rectangular top with a double row of stitching around the hem drops to just below the waist, and is worn over a thigh-length shirt, the back flap longer than the front one. The trousers are elasticated around the ankle and hand-painted in horizontal shadow stripes. All the garments feature utilitarian fabrics in contrasting textures, fashioned into square-shaped donkey jackets with bold patch pockets or ciré nylon crumpled tops and trousers. Sweaters of chunky knit and rib are patchworked with suede and felt, edges left raw, and worn over straight-legged trousers. The silhouette is layered throughout, comprising four or five components of loose-fitting geometric shapes in shades of black or cream.

London-based designer Green underpins his explorations into sculptural installations with a utilitarian approach to fashion that champions functionality, both in the choice of fabrics used and in the underlying structure of the garments. These offer contemporary leisurewear: minimally constructed pieces with a craft-based aesthetic and a sparing use of print and colour.

The creative freedom of menswear designers is now on a par with that of womenswear, with emerging designers such as Craig Green, Lee Roach and James Long exploring the genre without boundaries, preconceived ideas or gender stereotyping. Although Green presents a strong visual on the runway, without the bomb-blasted shed masks, the individual pieces ease into fluid, monochrome layers.

INDEX

PICTURE CREDITS

The publishers would like to thank the designers, photographers and museums for their kind permission to reproduce the works featured in this book. Every effort has been made to trace all copyright owners but if any have been inadvertently overlooked, the publishers would be pleased to make the necessary arrangements at the first opportunity.

2 Getty Images **10–11** Getty Images for IMG **13** Getty Images **17** © Condé Nast Archive / Corbis **18** Gamma-Keystone via Getty Images **21** REX / Sipa Press **22–23** © YURIKO NAKAO / Reuters / Corbis **25** Paris Match via Getty Images **26** Copyright Fergus Greer **28** © Reuters / Corbis **31** Pellerin / Photoshot **32** JB Villareal / Vogue.com **35** REX **37** firstVIEW **38** Tanausú Herrera **41** firstVIEW **43** Retna / Photoshot **44–45** WireImage **47** firstVIEW **48** Getty Images for IMG **51** AFP / Getty Images **52** Camera Press **55** REX /PIXELFORMULA / SIPA **56–57** WireImage **58** © Victoria and Albert Museum, London **61** © Howell Conant / Bob Adelman Books **63** The Metropolitan Museum of Art / Art Resource / Scala, Florence **64** © Condé Nast Archive / Corbis **67** © Fondation Pierre Bergé—Yves Saint Laurent / ph. Alexandre Guirkinger **68–69** © Julio Donoso / Sygma / Corbis **70** Gift of Hugo Boss, 1998 / The Metropolitan Museum of Art / Art Resource / Scala, Florence **72–73** Catwalking **74–75** Catwalking **76** firstVIEW **79** firstVIEW **81** UPPA / Photoshot **84** WireImage **87** Gamma-Rapho via Getty Images **88** Getty Images **91** © Derek Storm / Retna Ltd / Corbis **92** Pedro Reguera **95** FilmMagic **100** Catwalking **103** Getty Images **104** WireImage **107** Gorunway.com **108–109** REX / c J Tavin /Everett **110–111** REX / c.J Tavin / Everett **112** Getty Images **114** Mary Evans Picture Library / Interfoto **116–117** REX/Gunnar Larsen **119** photograph © Dennis Morris—all rights reserved **121** TopFoto.co.uk **122** firstVIEW **125** © Reuters / Corbis **126–127** Erik Madigan Heck **129** firstVIEW **133** firstVIEW **133** REX / Startraks Photo **134** Nikolaj Holm Møller **137** firstVIEW **138** Camera Press **141** © Kauffman / GoldenEye / Splash New s/ Corbis **142** Retna / Photoshot **144** Camera Press **146–147** firstVIEW **148** © Bettmann / Corbis **150–151** Time & Life Pictures / Getty Images **153** Getty Images **155** © Bettman / Corbis **156** WireImage **159** firstVIEW **160** firstVIEW **163** Gamma-Rapho via Getty Images **164** Camera Press **165** firstVIEW **168** firstVIEW **170** Josh Olins / Trunk Archive **173** AFP / Getty Images **174** Catwalking **176** Retna / Photoshot **179** firstVIEW **180–181** © FACUNDO ARRIZABALAGA / epa / Corbis **182** firstVIEW **184–185** Retna / Photoshot **187–188** AFP / Getty Images **191** Copyright The Museum at FIT **192** Copyright The Museum at FIT **195** firstVIEW **196** Gamma-Rapho via Getty Images **199** © Charles Platiau / Reuters / Corbis **200** © Fairchild Photo Service / Condé Nast / Corbis **202** Bloomberg via Getty Images **205** Getty Images **206** Retna / Photoshot **209** Getty Images **210** © Fairchild Photo Service / Condé Nast / Corbis **213** Retna / Photoshot **216** Retna / Photoshot **214–215** AFP / Getty Images

Quintessence would like to thank Caroline Eley for the index.

p.2: Rectangle dress by Agatha Ruiz de la Prada (see p.208)

First published in the United Kingdom in 2014 by
Thames & Hudson Ltd, 181A High Holborn,
London WC1V 7QX

© 2014 Quintessence Editions Ltd.

This book was designed and produced by
Quintessence Editions Ltd.
The Old Brewery, 6 Blundell Street,
London, N7 9BH

Editor	Becky Gee
Designer	Tom Howey
Editorial Assistant	Zoë Smith
Production Manager	Anna Pauletti
Editorial Director	Jane Laing
Publisher	Mark Fletcher

British Library Cataloguing-in-Publication Data
A catalogue record for this book is available from
the British Library

ISBN 978-0-500-29149-8

Printed in China

To find out about all our publications, please visit
www.thamesandhudson.com.
There you can subscribe to our e-newsletter, browse or download
our current catalogue, and buy any titles that are in print.